ALLAN JENKINS is editor of *Observer Food Monthly*. He was previously editor of the *Observer Magazine*, food and drink editor on the *Independent* newspaper and once lived in an experimental eco-community on Anglesey, growing organic food on the edge of the Irish sea. Allan's first book, *Plot 29*, was longlisted for the Baillie Gifford Prize and the Wellcome Book Prize.

Praise for *Morning*:

'A lovely read: illuminating conversations with early risers, from Jamie Oliver to dawn-seeking fishermen, interspersed with diary-style essays. It made me want to set my alarm a full hour earlier'   *Psychologies*

'In this philosophical hymn to the pleasure of waking early Allan Jenkins says that dawn is an enchanted world behind a hidden door, a time where you can be anybody you want to be, because the rest of the world is asleep ... it steadily becomes incredibly persuasive ... there's a golden period to do the things that are otherwise impossible in our busy lives. Seize the day indeed'

By the same author

Plot 29: A Memoir

MORNING
How To Make Time

ALLAN JENKINS

4th ESTATE • *London*

4th Estate
An imprint of HarperCollins*Publishers*
1 London Bridge Street
London SE1 9GF
www.4thEstate.co.uk

First published in Great Britain by 4th Estate in 2018
This 4th Estate paperback edition published 2019

1

A catalogue record for this book is
available from the British Library

ISBN 978-0-00-826437-6

Designed by BLOK www.blokdesign.co.uk

Printed and bound in Great Britain by
CPI Group (UK) Ltd, Croydon, CR0 4YY

MIX
Paper from
responsible sources
FSC www.fsc.org **FSC™ C007454**

This book is produced from independently certified FSC paper
to ensure responsible forest management.

Find out more about HarperCollins and the environment at
www.harpercollins.co.uk/green

For Henriette
For everything

Contents

Foreword

As cool as the pale wet leaves
of lily-of-the-valley
She lay beside me in the dawn
Ezra Pound, 'Alba'

For years now I have been getting up around 5 a.m. in winter (often earlier in summer). It suits me. I like the energy, the awareness before the day wakes. The quiet before dawn in winter, the shift from night to day in summer. I get things done. I write. I read. I think. I garden in soft light. It is my best time of day.

This short book will explore why.

I will make the case for being alert at first light. To wake in the quiet moments when the day inhales and the night fails. Just you and the stuff that surrounds you. To be extra alive in a way that near silence allows, sensitive to minute moments of change. To be able to gather yourself, your thoughts and feelings, whether it is to sit, to write, to walk, to read, to be inside or outside, to be sowing seed, to garden, to be saturated in experience. The gift of more time in the morning, so easily given and so easily missed. The simple opportunity to start the working day refreshed, renewed. To be whole in a way that near silence gives, to be one with the wild. To be natural in nature. To nurture yourself. The chance to be alive to your breath and distant from distraction. The space to be (by) yourself, before others wake.

It's easy, take it, half an hour, an hour, maybe more when you want. To be comfortable with yourself in a way that being alone allows no matter how many people you share your life with. The opportunity is there every day. Just you and the morning light, like flower or fauna. To learn to allow yourself to build in awareness, even if it's just of birdsong. To be awake in a moving meditation. Try it some time, take small steps, the morning world is waiting. You and the sky or a computer screen, the page of an unread book, the taste of tea. Bring the outside inside. The day can start when you want, uncoupled from demands and distraction. And if this doesn't work for you alone maybe find someone who wants to share the silence.

I will talk to a neuroscientist, a fisherman, a philosopher, painters and poets. I will interview other early morning people. I will examine how changes in light throughout the day, through the year, affect different people, plants. I will report on how time influences behaviour. I will take the first bus. I will report from different latitudes, including the Arctic Circle in summer (from barely three hours of daylight to twenty-four hours of sun) and the effects it has on inhabitants and me.

I will investigate the language of light and morning, the many words from different cultures for dawn and first light and what they mean and how they change.

I will keep an early morning diary from my window. I will describe how the light lifts, the sun rises, the birds sing or not throughout the year. I will observe and report. I will listen and feel.

I will tell the morning's story.

How to make time

Seize the day. Your morning doesn't have to be decided by what time you leave the house. The constant conventional rush: for breakfast, a bath or shower, in time for the bus or Tube or drive or walk to work, to get the kids to school. You can free the day, start in a different way, remove the race.

Build up to dawn, wake a little earlier, try half an hour. Skip *Newsnight* or Netflix, the phone the night before, or whatever it is you watch. They will still be there. Savour the time. Avoid doing the same you always do or the day will fill like an incoming tide. What is it you wanted to do but told yourself you don't have the time? Paint, possibly? Draw? Read more books? Bake bread? Do a little now. It's a start. Take baby steps.

Build on it, slowly if you need. Make it an hour earlier, build up to two, it's honestly even better, open space enough to think and feel. Don't rush it, take your time, you have enough.

Perhaps try to skip social or other media before you sleep and once you wake. Make your early day a holiday. It is easy, honestly.

If winter is too dark and daunting (though I think it is my favourite season), start in the spring, when the light will be there waiting, as will writing, reading, yoga, walking, sitting. Whatever it is you want.

Try having a window open, your eyes and ears, too. If it is dark use only low light. Sit near the window, let the outside in.

Free your morning and mind, later skip the electric light. You will know where you are, where to walk, what to do. You will have mapped out the space you are in. It's simple neuroscience.

Dark to light, an eternal transition, be alive to it sometime, aware, awake.

Don't beat yourself up if you skip it or feel the need to go back to bed. Build it in sometime. There is no right or wrong, only more opportunity. It is magical the morning. A forgiving friend. Yours, too, if you want.

A lexicon of dawn

Afrikaans: *aanbreek*

Azerbaijani: *sübh*

Basque: *egunsentian*

Bosnian: *zora*

Bulgarian: *разсъмване*

Catalan: *alba*

Corsican: *alba*

Croatian: *zora*

Czech: *úsvit*

Danish: *daggry*

Estonian: *koit*

French: *aube*

German: *Morgendämmerung*

Hawaiian: *ao*

Hungarian: *hajnal*

Icelandic: *dögun*

Irish: *breacadh an lae*

Italian: *alba*

Japanese: *Yoake*

Kurdish: *bandev*

Latvian: *ausma*

Lithuanian: *aušra*

Luxembourgish: *Sonnenopgang*

Malay: *subuh*

Maltese: *bidunett*

Maori: *ata*

Polish: *świt*

Portuguese: *amanhecer*

Romanian: *zori*

Russian: *рассвет*

Samoan: *vaveao*

Serbian: *зора*

Spanish: *alba*

Swahili: *alfajiri*

Swedish: *gryning*

Turkish: *şafak*

Urdu: *Sahar*

Welsh: *wawr*

Other usage

Old English
uhta
'the last part of the night, the time just before daybreak'.
Also *dagian*
verb, meaning 'to become day' (root of 'dawn', the time that
marks the beginning of twilight before sunrise)

Middle English, also Scots Gaelic
greking
'In the grekynge of the day, sir Gawayne hente his hors
wondyrs for to seke' (Malory, *Morte D'Arthur*)

Irish
le fáinne geal an lae
'the bright ring of the day'

French
l'heure bleue

Spanish
madrugar
verb, meaning, 'to get up early'
proverb, *Al que madruga, Dios le ayuda*, 'God helps those
who rise early'

US Pennsylvania Dutch
the blush

A manifesto

Early morning gives me time, hope, space. At a moment when they are all at a premium. The city (largely) sleeps. Interference is low, distractions minimal. My day opens up. Stretches languidly. My mind is clearer. My thoughts easier to read. Anxious urgency is removed. The light is almost elusive. I feel my way around, the room, my home. I become like a cat with whiskers. I pour tea. I fill the pot by sound not sight, a reassuring glug. It is curiously comforting to decouple from incessant electric light. I am aware of the air around me. I have hours on my own, free to follow my feelings. I am liberated from the day's demands. More at one, if you will, with the more natural world. Perhaps just sitting, watching my thoughts scroll by. I can write, walk, gaze out of the window, soak it in, enjoy it, luxuriate. There is time to wonder what I want to say. Time to drink good tea while people around me sleep. Time to hear the blackbird signal dawn (midsummer sunrise 4.42 a.m., London, and gone 8 a.m. by midwinter).

Early morning connects me, moves me, makes me more awake. I listen to more isolated sound while the day and light lift. My room more slowly makes its presence felt. My day, my world, knock politely. There is time to wait, rising sun on my face as I write. Cool light as I walk or garden, free from chatter, except my own, perhaps today a loop over Hampstead Heath, just me and the bumblebees, another early walker in the distance. I'll nod, quietly say hello if we pass, a brotherly sisterhood of sharing with other early morning appreciators. An hour's open-hearted meditation on morning, light and life. Stopping to admire the fading greening, perhaps catch sight of a solo heron. I am back before breakfast, in time to wake others up. Time to read, say, Ted Hughes's 'The Hawk in the Rain', to catch undone things from days before. Time to build in new memories, sow new seed.

From night to day, dark to dawn, winter to spring, there is enchantment for me in transition. This is when the owl flies, the curlew calls, the earth inhales or exhales. Flux, a natural thing. From boy to man, child to adult, it is in the letting go, watching, observing, not trying to control the change, where enchantment, even the miraculous, happens. Before breakfast was when I roamed by the river, ambled through fields and woods as a child, in search of young mushrooms and magic. Seeing the dog fox returning to his den, hearing the call of the wild, I knew anything, everything, was possible; reality's grip lessened for a moment and therein lay the charm. No longer defined by home or who my parents were, there were other possibilities on offer. Whatever I wanted. My imagination soared with the shift in light.

Decades later it still holds true. You can do near anything you want to, be almost anybody you want, the rest of the world is asleep. Loosen your shackles. For an hour or two feel free. There is nothing holding you back. Dawn is an enchanted world behind a hidden door, there if you want it, fine if you don't. 'Morning is when I am awake and there is a dawn in me,' says Thoreau. He's right.

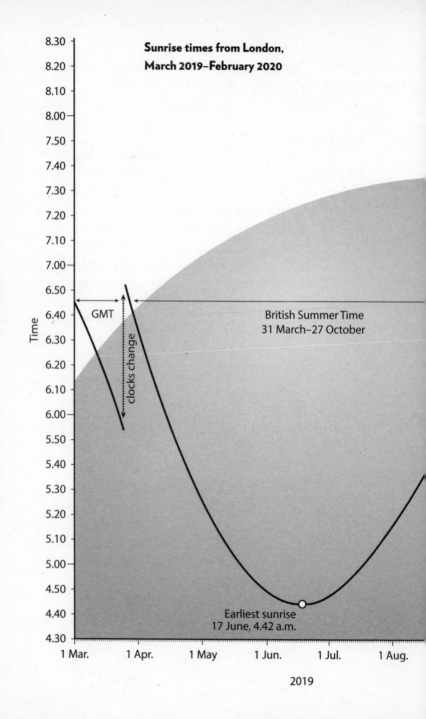

Sunrise times from London,
March 2019–February 2020

GMT

clocks change

British Summer Time
31 March–27 October

Earliest sunrise
17 June, 4.42 a.m.

Time

8.30
8.20
8.10
8.00
7.50
7.40
7.30
7.20
7.10
7.00
6.50
6.40
6.30
6.20
6.10
6.00
5.50
5.40
5.30
5.20
5.10
5.00
4.50
4.40
4.30

1 Mar.   1 Apr.   1 May   1 Jun.   1 Jul.   1 Aug.

2019

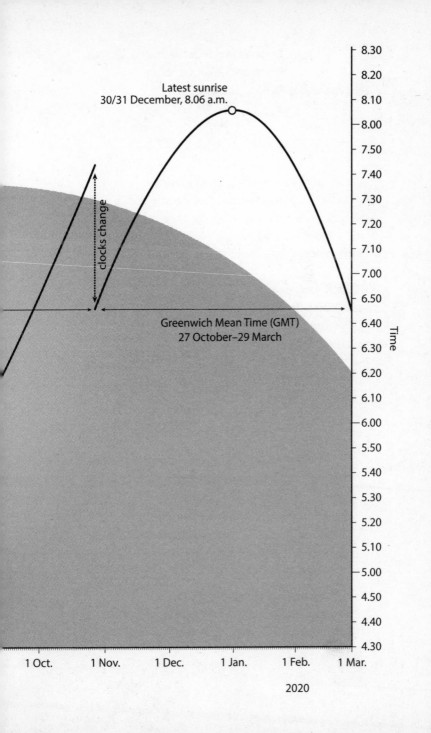

Latest sunrise
30/31 December, 8.06 a.m.

clocks change

Greenwich Mean Time (GMT)
27 October–29 March

Time

8.30
8.20
8.10
8.00
7.50
7.40
7.30
7.20
7.10
7.00
6.50
6.40
6.30
6.20
6.10
6.00
5.50
5.40
5.30
5.20
5.10
5.00
4.50
4.40
4.30

1 Oct.   1 Nov.   1 Dec.   1 Jan.   1 Feb.   1 Mar.

2020

My morning: Allan Jenkins

First, could you tell me a little about yourself?
I am a writer, an editor, a gardener. At twenty, as a single
parent, I could sometimes skip sleep completely if, say, my
young daughters were unwell. Now I need maybe seven
hours, perhaps a nap at the weekend.

What time do you wake up (and why)?
Some time before 5 a.m. in summer, a little later in winter.
I sleep with sliding doors open, no curtains. It is usually the
birds that wake me, even gulls a joyful thing. It is the time
I write or summer-garden, though I sometimes get caught
up in social media, before my wife gets up.

Do you have a morning ritual?
I like to make tea in the dark. I think my senses may be
heightened. Earl Grey in a pot, no milk.

How does being awake early affect your life?
It gives me time to be me, before the day begins.

What time do you sleep?
Mostly around ten-ish, give or take.

Does your sleep vary through the year?
I am up earlier in summer, more energetic, more excitable
and so are the birds. I don't know that I get more done.

Has your sleep pattern changed?
Maybe less sleep with age, though it is more likely I have
carved out time to write and/or garden that I don't have in
the evening when I need to cook and digest the day.

Is the light important?
It is everything. I think I am addicted. The shift from night,
the sometimes timid start of day. My world wakes.
Particularly if there is sun, of course. I write by an open
window facing south-east; the light draws me outside,
catches the vase of flowers beside me (there are always
flowers). Most mornings I take a photo, same photo, same
view, of the sunrise. I tell myself it is like Monet's water
lilies or haystacks but I think I am mapping my life
in mornings.

What do you like least about being awake early?
I can lose an hour reading useless links to politics or old
YouTube, purely because I can.

What do you like best about being awake early?
The energy, the time it gives; it feels like a gift (apologies for
romance but it is true). Sometimes it allows me to escape to
the allotment, feed it, water it, sow seeds, connect with land
and wild.

*How would you sum up your thoughts on your mornings in
100 words or less?*
Sometimes I feel it is my secret, like Narnia, outside time or
at least the rest of the day. I cannot believe everyone doesn't
know about it and take an occasional step through the
wardrobe.

My morning: Jamie Oliver

First, could you tell me a little about yourself?
My name is Jamie Oliver, I'm a chef, writer and child health campaigner. I was born in 1975 in Southend, Essex. I have five fantastic kids and live mainly in north London.

What time do you wake up (and why)?
Work days I tend to wake up at 4.45 a.m. by my phone and the gentle music of a band called Aqualung. Saying that, I've normally switched it off within three seconds. I get up that early because I start official work at 7.30 a.m., where time is planned within an inch of its life, so if I want to go to the gym or squeeze a meeting in that can't wait I use early mornings as my trump card to do what I want. I find it really useful. If I was off work and didn't have kids jumping on me I probably could easily lie in. I don't remember when that last happened.

Do you have a morning ritual?
I tiptoe to my bathroom where I fill a big bath with hot water full to the brim with a squeeze of Johnson's purple baby bubble bath which I've taken a shine to. I have a thing about the ritual of the bath. I found my dream tub in a scrapyard eighteen years ago: a lucky find, Clarice Cliff made it, solid porcelain. The bath is my only quiet time, true relaxation, to relieve my aching muscles. I take thirty minutes to try to think and visualise my day ahead. I then pack my clothes, get in my gym gear and run, cycle or scooter to the gym.

How does being awake early affect your life?
I think it arms me to be more productive, more creative, gives me a head start that I feel I need as many people look to me for answers and clarity from 7.30 a.m. onwards so I need to start before others tend to. The effect is, I think, you have a different rhythm, maybe it feels like a cheat. I crave early morning peace and quiet and space for thought and to appreciate nature, particularly birds singing. Dad used to wake me up early as a kid, he said people died in bed – so I guess it's stuck.

What time do you sleep?
I go to bed about 10 p.m. if I can and I sleep very well, but actually physically going to bed is one of my hardest challenges in the day. I think there's always so many reasons not to just go to bed, so like a baby I set my watch to remind me to get in bed. Pathetic, but it works really well.

Does your sleep vary through the year?
No, it's always the same unless I'm on holiday when I tend to chill out more and have a lie in.

Has your sleep pattern changed?
Yes. I used to get sleep very wrong. I didn't understand it or respect it, I took it for granted like a luxury not a necessity. I only used to get three or so hours' sleep for about six years, which got me in the end. For the first time I felt really sad, which has never been my default as I'm a very positive person most of the time so I had to change my thinking and doing this has changed my life. Sleep is as important as nutrition.

Is the light important?
Oh yeah, I crave a little kiss of sun, it feels like a charge, comfort, joy. I'll follow light like I follow the smell of good food, never direct light unless it's sunrise or sunset. To have a power nap facing autumn orange light on your face is true luxury joy.

What do you like least about being awake early?
The fear of waking up the kids and especially the baby.

What do you like best about being awake early?
The chance to be one step ahead of most.

How would you sum up your thoughts on your mornings in 100 words or less?
My early mornings are a lonely, self-indulgent, special space that I choose to create for myself because we can. Where time goes at normal speed instead of fast forward.

Dawn diary

The little violets' heads bowed on their stems,
The pre-dawn gossamers, all dew and scrim
And star-lace
Seamus Heaney, Mycenae Lookout, 'His Dawn Vision'

| 1 March | 6 March | 20 March | 21 March |
| Sunrise 6.46 a.m. | New moon | Vernal equinox | Full moon |

MARCH

31 March
Sunrise 6.39 a.m.

March 1

4.05 a.m., London

First day of meteorological spring. Sunrise calculated: 6.45 a.m. I read, I write, I make tea. By 5 a.m. the back-garden blackbird's song is less shouty, more melodious. There are runs, there is sweetness. It feels tender, personal. I wonder if he can see me from my open window, face picked out in the screen light. It's still too dark to see him. Maybe there is an appreciative female, maybe as yet there is only me. It is quiet, just my fingers quietly rat-tatting on the computer keyboard, him and his sweet song.

March 6

5 a.m.

Is it the streetlight out the front that makes the church bird sing? I lie in bed listening through the open doors but Henri's sleeping breath is anxious. I cuddle her until it calms. My dawn writing feels like a series. The fascination of recording almost invisible change. Here I sit at my window. Noting the subtle shift.

I miss an early bus to the plot, watch it pass as I am putting on my boots. I am still on site before seven. Here to sow the first root crops of spring. One row each of red beetroot and Chioggia, marked by blue string. The rain starts as I am sowing. I love its gentle touch. The ponds are alive with bulbous spawn.

It's a double bakery shop today. First, the French for pastry, another for cinnamon buns. I am home and armed with breads and papers before my daughter Kala, who lives close by, comes around for breakfast.

March 7

5.20 a.m.

Cooler at the window, as I write. Daybreak gathering,
mauve clouds to the south, steel sky north-east,
watercolour streaks at twelve o'clock. Crows are adding
bass notes to the small-bird choir. It is almost light at
6.10 a.m., skies a dirty denim. Is it mad to say I miss the dark
in the mornings? I sowed five rows of spring seed on
Sunday, so they need light and warmth, and me too, but
now winter is weaker I feel some slight regret. It might be a
cocoon thing, anyway it will soon pass. The anemones by
the screen no longer need monitor light, their chiffon petals
picked out in subdued daylight.

March 8

3.28 a.m.

So now I know when the church blackbird first calls.
Incessant rain had woken me, then the chorus began. There
is a joy there, in rain and song that breaks through any
mood. No neighbouring house lights anywhere. People
asleep as far as I can see. Just me and my tuneful feathered
friends. I love being wrapped in this quarter-light. There is
comfort to be found in doing nothing much, breathing,
aware of the early day, the almost silence in a city.

March 10

2.28 a.m.

Back home after being trapped on a broken train, a three-
hour journey taking ten. Stepping out of the cab, ready for
bed, to be greeted by the blackbird singing as though only
for me. The mystery of the song and when it starts. I pause
for a minute, soak it in, stand under its shower, and then
haul myself up the stairs.

March 11

4.30 a.m.

The dark has gone as the near-full moon waxes. Birdsong in surround sound. I read a poem about kindness. The sun when it comes is a watercolour primrose. A Japanese start to its day.

March 13

4.08 a.m.

Woken by full moon and birdsong streaming through the doors. March is known as the sap moon or worm moon, signalling warming soil where worms re-emerge and bring migrating birds back to feed. The kitchen smells of scented narcissi. Spring is very close. The sky is shrugging off its winter coat, full-on streaming sunrise.

March 15

3.50 a.m.

Henri has to get up at 4 a.m., leave the house at five, so of course I wake early, the same with any flight day, birthday, Christmas Day. While she packs, I pootle about, making breakfast, running her bath. Two blackbirds are locked in a song contest, early geese and swans fly by, plaintive calls of long haul. The ranunculus in the jug look like a kid's painting. The 5.30 a.m. sky is streaked with pink lipstick air trails. Henri is not the only one to fly.

March 17

4.45 a.m.

I am lying diagonally on the bed, my sleeping legs seeking my absent wife. Kentish Town is marked out in birdsong, trees hosting answering calls, like echoes in a canyon, beacons on a cliff. A dawn dialogue, the tribal chat. I wonder whether they've paired yet or is it like ducks on the canal: five males for every anxious female. The blackbird

boundaries are hardening for the breeding season.
From now until July their small town territories will be
fiercely defended. As yet the call feels melodic rather
than aggressive.

By 6 a.m. I am sowing beans and nasturtiums at the
allotment at the top of Hampstead. The hill is an avenue of
birdcall. One sings from scaffolding profiled against the
breaking day. The sunrise catches the willow branches. The
pink magnolia is coloured bubblegum. By 7.30 a.m. I am
home, elated, making breakfast. Soon the rest of the house
will wake.

March 18
5.15 a.m.
I have been up extra early reading 'Love after Love' by Derek
Walcott, who has just died. Then into Seamus Heaney, as it
was St Patrick's Day yesterday. Henri calls from upstairs.
She is having trouble sleeping. I climb into bed and curl
into her. The poetry of quiet breath as her rhythm slows.

March 21
5.21 a.m.
Blue sky, spring dawn; we are past the equinox (equal
night) now; for the first time in six months the day will be
(just) longer than the dark. The sun creeps up behind its
temporary home. The tower block lit with hope. Crows
shout their welcome, magpies mock. Early light catches the
rosemary flowers in the window box. Still before 7 a.m. and
the sun has real warmth. A day to sow salad seed.

March 22
5.03 a.m.
Turner-esque streaky sky. The neighbour's cat comes in off
the roof, scratching at the door. She doesn't want to stay,
she doesn't want to talk. She trots through the flat, down

three flights and sits impatient, calling to be let out into the street. I watch for a few moments, see she is safe and mourn the days she came to stay.

My mornings create space to let my mood materialise, listen to myself without distraction. Like a flower adjusting to the sun, knowing which way I want to face. The room adjusts, too, takes on a glow, the flowers take on a different tone: green stems stand out in red.

The sky's reflected in the western window, mirroring the morning. Like a planet with two suns, bathing me in ambient light. It is not, I think about what you do in the early morning – though there are more opportunities with extra hours – it is about giving yourself me-moments, the simple gift of time. Liberated from urgency, revealing the joy of being you, unleashed like a lurcher in a meadow, all in your front room. It mostly comes with sunrise. And it's still only 6.30 a.m.

March 25
4.33 a.m., Denmark

First, to light the fire (as always), then time for tea. By 5 a.m. the blackbirds sing. I wonder whether they have a Scandinavian accent. Within moments the hedges are alive, my tea mug steams, the flames lick at the logs. Within half an hour it's seven degrees outside, a full twelve up on yesterday. It feels like this is the end of the frost. I am sowing spring flower seed. No sunrise through the trees today, a slow creeping in of dawn. By 5.45 a.m. there is a smear on the east horizon. Light is coming fast. I can see my writing on the page. Ink. No computer screen here. The last day of winter light. Tonight the clocks spring forward. The sun rises, silvered. A palest gold picks out the pennant on a neighbour's flagpole. The birds chatter. The woodpecker drums.

March 26

4.06 a.m., Denmark

First day of summer, two hours on from GMT. The eastern sky has a platinum tint, newly shiny. It's quiet, still, no sound from the sea. Within an hour, birdsong is everywhere, with many on the move. The Arctic terns are leaving, the lapwings have arrived. Resident crows, the finches, tits, all compete in the choir. I wish I knew more of their songs. Light softens as the temperature drops. Quickly down to two degrees. In an incoming sea mist the thrush song is suddenly isolated, the collared doves cacophonic.

March 27

5.05 a.m., London, back to being dark

The extra summer hour in the evening has robbed my morning light. Backwards, forwards, as though we think we have control of time. The day is on hold, you can still wake and see the sunrise. It is easier now it is later, at least for a week or two. More time to quietly contemplate, more time to write in screen light. Though we have just made later earlier, the opportunity to step outside time is still on offer if we want to slow down time. The 7 a.m. neighbour leaves his door at 6.30 a.m. today. The sun is quickly catching its stolen hour. Rising hidden now behind a new building. Sky trails bomb the tower block. A palette of blues and electric oranges, rich like Rubens.

March 31

5.05 a.m.

Crazy birdsong all around, everyone joins in. The magpies across the street pairing now, either renewing their courtship or making friends. Multiple mating calls the order of the day. In Denmark they are mostly comically in twos, seabirds too, and gulls. Flirting, flying, aware of the need to attach. I am almost anxious to get the early bus, the seed peas downstairs call for soil. It is the time of growth, of new life, of seed spilled and spread and germination. It seems I share spring urgency. In the garden a cat calls, deep and intent.

My morning: Jane Domingos

First, could you tell me a little about yourself?
I am Jane, born 1964. I like to describe myself as a 'creative'.
I have been able to observe and draw accurately as long as I
can remember and took the ability for granted until
relatively late in life. I have excess creative energy that
excites and frustrates in equal measure.

What time do you wake up (and why)?
I wake up before any alarms go off in the house, usually
around 6 a.m. but it can be 5 a.m. For the past two years I've
been waking up at the time my father died. He confounded
everybody by living three weeks without sustenance
beyond the day they expected him to die. I had sat all night
with him the day he finally passed away. It was early
morning in the care home and the day staff had just arrived.
It was as if Dad took all the paraphernalia of the night
including the medics and staff and all manner of other
night creatures with him. Never has the contrast between
the night and day been so stark for me. It was August and
dawn had happened unnoticed behind the thick blackout
curtains of his institutional room. Daylight seemed too
sudden and the business of a new day too soon. It took me
a couple of weeks to realise I was waking at the time of
his death.

A similar thing had happened as a child after finding my
elderly and ill grandmother passed away one morning. I'd
gone in with her cup of tea and found her cold. For a couple
of years after I would wake up suddenly at four fifteen

every morning and stare at my door expecting someone to come in. My bedroom was always dark, being fitted with 1970s dark brown velvet curtains. My imagination ran wild and I wondered if maybe that had been the time she died.

Do you have a morning ritual?
On waking I always look first towards the natural light, which is usually a window. For several years we had a bedroom that faced north but I would leave the door ajar so that the morning light would fall through from a landing window on the other side of the house. I would look at this light rather than the window in the room and on a sunny morning the sunlight would be prettily refracted through an old cut-glass doorknob. Even in a room with a heavily curtained window I will seek out a chink of daylight before doing anything else.

I then check my phone for the time, news headlines and any notifications. I try hard at this point to resist the urge to click on anything. I go to the bathroom but have rarely committed to actually 'getting up' early. I think I used to feel slightly worried about being up and about before anyone else in the house or maybe worried that I wasn't getting enough sleep. On occasions when I have woken early enough and the glow in the eastern sky looks promising of a good sunrise or there is frost or snow on the ground then I'll dress properly and head out for a walk through streets or over fields. Occasionally I drive to a spot where I particularly want to see the dawn working its magic.

We recently moved to a house with a smaller garden and a fox lair. I look for them out the window on rising and if they are there or if I am hopeful they will be there at some point, then I silently make my way down an extension to the rear and side of the house that takes me to within a few feet of where they are playing or sniffing for food. They seem oblivious to me standing at the window and I watch enthralled, their coats and eyes particularly stunning in the dawn light.

How does being awake early affect your life?
Being awake early forces me to acknowledge my individuality. I always feel energised and, unless particularly in the depths of a depression, hopeful the new day will bring good things. It is a time of much internal dialogue. For me, watching the sun rise or set causes an emotion I don't feel at any other time. Finally, at some point I experience a kind of disappointment when I realise the sun is up above the clouds and we are fully lit – the illumination has been rapid but subtle.

What time do you sleep?
Lights out for many years has been 1.30 a.m. I worry it is too late. At night I value time alone after everyone else has gone to sleep and find it amazingly productive. I write thoughts down and make lists for the day ahead. I check my diary.

Does your sleep vary through the year?
Whether it's winter or summer I always feel a need to be out of doors if the sun is out. I really don't like grey summer days and feel angry at something but don't know what. In the winter I accept the gloom and feel quite happy to busy myself with work or curl up with a book. Nightfall in the winter excites me as much as daybreak in the summer.

Has your sleep pattern changed?
When the children were young I would start work after they went to bed and could easily work through to 2 a.m. and still be up early for the school run. Now that I am older and since being ill I fall asleep in the evening.

Is the light important?
It is vital. Apart from needing sunlight for health and wellbeing, as an artist it helps me to understand the world. Strong directional light is what transforms an object from appearing two-dimensional to three-dimensional. Seen in sunlight the world pings into focus with depth and distance and a richness of colour. However tired, I am always reluctant to sleep if the sun is shining.

What do you like least about being awake early?
There isn't anything I don't like about being awake early. I know I am free to crawl back into bed at any point I choose.

What do you like best about being awake early?
Having a good night's sleep is a recharge of your batteries. Having a good night's sleep and being awake at dawn is the icing on the cake – a lithium battery as opposed to alkaline.

How would you sum up your thoughts on your mornings in 100 words or less?
On a good day, and preferably a sunny one, mornings are a fresh start, a new opportunity. Energised, I feel ready and able to tackle anything and I look forward to creating something new. Joe Wright's 2005 film adaptation of *Pride and Prejudice* is a family favourite. The final scene, as the lovers are drawn into the new day before the world is awake, nails dawn beautifully. Rising sun, pale lemony light, dawn chorus, a meadow, dissipating mist, clarity of thought and vision, hope on the horizon, the promise of something new, and love, of course, always love.

1 April
Sunrise 6.36 a.m.

5 April
New moon

19 April
Full moon

30 April
Sunrise 5.35 a.m.

APRIL

April 1

3.06 a.m.

The owl wakes me. An ancient-seeming sound in a busy urban street, disconnected almost from it. Lordly. Its call calls, if you will, summons me from sleep. I am here, it says, worth being awake for. I wonder who it talks to. Is there a sparse network of other owls? As a child I used to watch them fly by my window, spirits I saw. They talk in secrets, a lonely call as code. I am glad to wake and hear it before I go back to sleep for an hour, get up at 4.20 a.m., dress in the semi-dark. The blackbird kicks back in just gone five, a showier showing-off song. It fills the gardens. More comfortable, almost more middle class, sort of suburban.

By 5.50 a.m. I am at the allotment, the fruit trees are in blossom, the apple blossom ghost-lit in the gloom. The baby broad beans are darker-green shadows against the earth. The cardoons are rushing, the forget-me-nots are covering in carpets. It is not yet light. The sunrise catches chicory, like paper-wrapped red bunches of flowers. I sow a couple of rows of radish. I mostly sit and listen. Suddenly it is 7 a.m., time to buy fish and oranges, fresh bread for breakfast.

April 3

5.55 a.m.

Gathering thoughts and drinking tea, start of the week. Reading world news before 6 a.m. and back to yoga. It has been a while and feels like it. My hamstrings tell me. It is good to be back on the mat, my wife on my left. Her shoulder is bettering. We both groan a bit and grin. We salute the nearly there sun and stretch. We bend, we shape like cobras, we do spinal twists. We breathe consciously.

April 5

4.10 a.m.

The city almost sleeps, almost silence, just the background thrum of 10 million people breathing. By 5.05 a.m. sirens are screaming, birdsong is agitated, London is woke. Well, some of it; mostly me and the emergency crews, cops, paramedics mopping up last night's emergencies, making today's arrests.

April 6

5.25 a.m.

The owl appears to have moved into the churchyard. Its call as yet only tentative (I think it may be adolescent), it hands over at the end of its shift to the blackbirds. The bird of night and the bird of morning, outside my London window, calling the passing day, matins and vespers, the hours as holy service.

April 9

3.20 a.m.

Woken by a bright moon. The French windows wide open, it is quiet outside, just the spring morning cool creeping through. Swedes call this time *Vargtimmen*, the hour of the wolf: the time between night and dawn when the wild is said to be outside your door, usually thought to be between 3 a.m. and 5 a.m. It is used to describe 'an organism that is only active in the pre-dawn hours or early morning', less likely wolves than bees now looking to escape competition for pollen. Some flowers, such as morning glory, have adapted to this practice. Increasingly it almost describes me.

April 13

3.40 a.m., Denmark

Even here on the Danish coast where the sun sets late and rises close to 4 a.m., it's the blackbird that overrides sleep. Here is magic, he sings, forget your day job, your duties, here you too are like me, alive, awake, alert. I can almost hear the first sun hit the top leaf, see the gentle bathing, feel the day's soft touch. The house is scented with summer lilac, picked from the path. Hedges of variations, a softened violet, churned with cream. The fragrance of Nordic summer, everywhere, dotted through every road. A punctuation of place. This is Denmark, it says, in a way the blackbird can't with its universal sing-song.

The sun breaks through the branches at 4.10 a.m., a laser pulse of yellow light. Soon it catches doors, trees, casts watery shadows, branches are rewritten. The tall trees bathe in it like last night's dew. This is the day's first food. The oak warms, changes colour, shrugs off the gloom. Here is rejuvenation, renewal, refreshment. Fast now. Urgent. It runs through the leaves. The northern sun in its pomp, life-giving, nutritional, heat for the later harvest, sunlight for growth, for baby birds, for the blossom, bees. A pollination of the day, touching everything everywhere, moving on. Here I am part of the process, waiting to be lit. I gather thoughts, harvest them, scythe them down, rake them up, for compost, for pillows for picnics: green and sappy, to be dried and used later for fuel.

April 15

4.55 a.m.

A black and white light. Charred sheen on the terrace. Trees silhouetted, the wood a solid charcoal sketch. Blocks of near black for nearby houses. Almost total silence broken at 5.20 a.m. by birds. Suddenly they are all in song. I wonder how long they have been wondering whether to sing.

A wall of sound, maybe a hedge, but no species dominant, all in full flow, bass treble, soprano sections. No long solos, every bird has its part. The rain like a percussion track taps on the metal chimney of the stove, lays down a back rhythm on the terrace. The fire joins in with a liquid roar, like wind, like waves.

Within half an hour the birds quiet, still singing but more sidetracked, as though they have things to do, babies to feed. The tunes change, become more reedy. The yellow flowering bush is lit, the monochrome filled in. Soft edges. Shadows. The grass a fat green brushstroke, more for the idea than the thing, no detail as yet, the mood of grass, a signal. White wood anemones almost shine in the meadow, perhaps a pearl necklace.

April 20
5.15 a.m., London
Slept in, late night. The back gardens are full of cats. The black-and-white Felix is the most fearless, the one who gets trapped in trees and on roofs. He is stalking another smaller, younger cat like him. The dog behind the fence makes a lunge as he passes. Both cats quickly disappear. A new tabby sits on a far elevated corner, looking down, studying its new world. The dominant black stalks the flat roof with a swagger.

This is the big cat-meeting place, four or more with their own corners, some like time-shares, the youngest sometimes looking to play or engage. They jump from roof to roof like Spiderman, walk long narrow fences like acrobats. Acutely aware of each other but mostly respectful. Except Felix. Within half an hour they have ducked away and disappeared through flaps in search of breakfast and sleep.

Eight crows suddenly sit in the tallest church tree, like an unsettling omen. An oddly quiet invasion. One launches and lazily leads five others away. A couple stay for some personal time.

April 21
4.10 a.m.
The church blackbird exultant as I lie awake. Sings for an hour, almost exactly, and stops. Moments later, another starts out the back (or is it the same bird on another boundary edge?). Within a few minutes, stereo, but both songs further away. All the while, the crescent moon, clear as day. By 5.20 a.m. I can see details, apple blossom, lilac, white windows. The sky is colouring over Canary Wharf.

April 26
5.05 a.m.
Blackbird of course, fast-moving clouds, cold. A kind of muddy tint to the sky. But it is light now. It feels like I am using fewer of my senses. My eyes greedily mop up all the information, my hearing less so. It's as though I don't 'feel' the invisible magic of the morning as much. The blossom is fading, the London lilac kicking in. Kala's rose is blooming, the rosemary flowers are fading fast. The bees have moved on to more choices.

By 6.15 a.m. the dawn chorus is exhausted, Henri's alarm goes off. The call for yoga. Ducks fly past in military formation, necks outstretched like fighter aircraft; they buzz the house, honking loudly. There is joy in the sound. Scraps of sky blue show through. A man in black stands smoking on a terrace. He looks left and right, sucks deeply. He is replaced by a woman. The question as to why they don't smoke together is answered when they re-emerge together a few minutes later carrying their baby down the stairs.

April 27

4.35 a.m.

Three thunderous bangs rip me from sleep. Seismic. Did the house shake? It feels like an invasion, an attack on its foundations. My heart thumps. Was it a bomb, someone breaking in? Again, a series of thuds. Shouting! A woman's voice. Fear and anger. It's a door being attacked. A family trying to hold out. A man trying to get into his home. A partner determined to stop him. The door holds. He attacks, screams his frustration. She screams her rage. Neighbours appear on balconies. Disturbed. Concerned. Curious.

The police arrive. The shouting almost stops. For a while. An hour and a half later the cops are still there, some milling outside, fretful, stuck, perhaps bored. Most everyone else tries to sleep. It's not the first time. Most of the police leave by 6.30 a.m. One stays, constantly on his phone until I go to work. Otherwise quiet.

April 28

4.22 a.m.

No bangs just maybe silence that woke me. There is something reassuring about being back awake in the half light, filling the teapot by sound, hearing the birds start to sing, seeing the pots of daisy and lily of the valley grey in the gloom. The blackbirds are more modest, part of a small band not a choir. One each, commanding front and back. At the moment, the church bird feels dominant. The first neighbouring light comes on at 5.19 a.m., mood subdued. An orange hue at daybreak, smothered by sunrise; all that is left is a pale peachy tone to the room.

My morning: Guy Grieve

First, could you tell me a little about yourself?
I'm a dive fisher for king scallops working from the Isle of
Mull, Inner Hebrides, off the west coast of Scotland.

What time do you wake up (and why)?
I wake up just before or by dawn in time to get my boat and
crew out to sea by first light. Dive fishing, swimming for
king scallops underwater, is all about sharp sight. And so
like all animals that rely on their eyesight to live I need as
much of the day as possible. Sometimes I also need to get to
sea early enough to allow for long journeys to remote reefs
and coastlines where we hope to find scallops.

Do you have a morning ritual?
At home, on a dark winter's morning with wind and rain
invariably falling, I often lie quite still for a while judging
from what direction the wind is blowing. An intimate chart
of the waters that surround my island home unravels and
I start to think about where we can risk taking the boat. I
also almost always tell myself that the hardest part of the
day is getting up.

Once the stove is lit, the boat's kettle is set to boil as the
engine warms and, sadly, tobacco is rolled as we huddle
in the wheelhouse and decide which course to steer for
the day.

How does being awake early affect your life?
I see things that enrich me. The deer moving up from the grass beside my loch to the higher ground. The greylag geese and their young sipping fresh water from the burn before returning to the foreshore. Herons finding their hunting stand for the morning and seals lumbering about on their precarious roosts amid rocks nearly awash. I'm allowed a glimpse of the wilderness around me waking. To get the fullness of a day is to be allowed more hours of life.

What time do you sleep?
When I'm working I try to be under covers by 10 p.m.

Does your sleep vary through the year?
In the summer, early light around 4 a.m. will make me turn over when I'm not diving. I have no curtains or blinds. In the winter I might sleep later, if the clock is not set, as light only comes at around 9 a.m.

Has your sleep pattern changed?
Two things in turn have messed with my sleep pattern. First children and after this, starting my own fishing business vanquished my early hours' tranquillity.

Is the light important?
Light is everything. Dive fishing is a sharp-eyed game and light levels are vital, even in the winter when it's so dark we don't even see the seabed as we sink, until it hits us. In the winter our mornings are spent in darkness as we head to the boat and often as we steam out to the fishing grounds. Daylight is spent on the water and we return in darkness.

What do you like least about being awake early?
The sense that sleep has been relegated to a practical sphere and not allowed to become an indulgence.

What do you like best about being awake early?
It's the world before mankind has fucked it up.

How would you sum up your thoughts on your mornings in 100 words or less?
The morning sets the mood of the day's diving to come. My work is dominated by the sea and weather and so the mornings are a time of portent. I always look hard at the sky and think about wind strength and direction. One day I long to be woken by wind and rain hitting my window before dawn and for it to be OK. For there to be no need for me to pull myself out from shelter and into the weather. To just be able to sleep through it all and to wake when the comfortable people wake.

1 May	4 May	18 May	31 May
Sunrise 5.33 a.m.	*New moon*	*Full moon*	*Sunrise 4.50 a.m.*

May 5

4.25 a.m.

Mackerel-skin sky on the horizon. It has been cloudy and cold for a week now, the first in May, not many breaks in daybreak. I close a window, shut out the chill to discover I have disturbed a silent bird. Sitting on the sill, two feet away, sharing the morning with me. By 5.05 a.m. the horizon is showing pale colour, warmer hues among the greys, almost a seascape. I am aware of the trees on the skyline in a way I wasn't much before. More confident, more assertive. Sunrise clears the sky by 6 a.m., almost a different day.

May 7

3.45 a.m., International Dawn Chorus Day

BBC Radio 4 is broadcasting birdsong throughout the night, following dawn as it journeys from India. Thousands of people around the world are joining in group events. The only London gathering is far away south and I want my chorus uninterrupted by crowds.

I am at the allotment at 4.10 a.m., passing three teenagers heading home, a man with a walking stick walking his dog. At the gates of the allotments, the birds on the street-lit borders are already wide awake. An owl calls from deep in the woods. Tulips are picked out in the electric light from the stairs. Bamboo structures stand out in the creeping light.

By 4.25 a.m. the blackbird calls from the wooded corner. Song surrounds me now. I record for the record, occasionally tuning into the radio for the bitterns and geese on the marsh. By 4.40 a.m. the white tulips loom in natural light. Crows cross the breaking sky. By 4.50 a.m. the first pigeon coos and I can see my writing for the first time. The silhouettes are stronger. By 5 a.m. the crows are croaking and the blackbirds are darting on the ground. A woman is singing in a wetland on Radio 4.

I sit contented for another hour, connected by the joy of dawn to twitchers, insomniacs and other early risers.

May 11
5.25 a.m.
Late night, later morning, though up in time to catch the sunrise. The sky is crisp, clear, dissected by a single jet streak pointing east. The morning doesn't mind I am later, waiting, patient, like a school friend or pet to see if I want to play. It is almost an acceptance. Time is (of course) indifferent. But in the way that I believe land can recognise me, plants grow for me, share a relationship, then it is not hard to extend that to morning: a welcome there if you want it, an acknowledgement perhaps. Clearer communication, an energy shift, like a space that has just been cleaned, a screen that has been wiped, a body freshly bathed. Sun shines. It is early summer. A police siren calls.

May 13
12.30 a.m.
Woken by cramp and late chocolate. I lie an hour listening to Henri's regular breathing. By 2.05 a.m. a lone gull circles, its plaintive call echoed by an owl. At 2.30 a.m. I get up, make tea and peace with the night. I decide to test an earlier dawn chorus. To map the morning. At 3.19 a.m. a cat growls. A neighbouring light goes out. Someone's decided it's time to sleep. I wash and dress. It's the weekend, I will likely nap later. The sky is slightly red, the rooftop daisies a ball of almost white in almost light but early bird call calls.

I phone a cab to the allotment. No time to walk. There is no one around. All quiet.

Plot, 3.37 a.m., silence, just trees rustling, a distant car. I passed only two others in two miles. There is no active animal life. Just me. I will sow flower seed before I leave.

A first, dawn sowing. There is a rusty sound like a sign swinging.

The first call comes at 3.49 a.m. It is halting, almost whispered. Tiny, tentative. There is no answer. At 3.53 a.m. I hear the first song; 3.55 a.m. the first response. An owl calls back at 3.57 a.m. and there are now four birds in play. It is light enough to wander around. The blackbird sings at 4.07 a.m., then the first follows from the unlit wood. A train calls, lonesome; a motorbike accelerates. The bird call moves closer from darker trees. A small cloud of crows join in.

It is light enough to sow. I move tear peas from the nursery bed. I lay out five short rows for seed. I sow red *Tagetes* Ildkonge in memory of my brother. Because I love him and them. I sow yellow summer squash to spill down the bank.

I sit and soak in shifts in light and song. I absorb the almost quiet. Dawn bathing, I call it. Natured. Nurtured. Energy-topped like late sun on a beach, a morning walk on moorland, sitting by a stream. I charge. Refill my battery. Still my heart.

Before 6 a.m. I leave for the fishmonger. He is boiling crabs outside. He grins, says he has been thinking about me and a Mrs Levy. It's the first sea trout of the year, he says. I buy his fish and samphire. Dinner will taste of summer. I walk past the scavenging pigeons sorting through fox-spilled bin bags. Fixated, they ignore me as I pass. The good greengrocer down the hill is setting out his stall. I buy three white peaches. Home before seven, I have slept an hour but feel refreshed.

May 21

4.40 a.m.

Back in my London bed after being in Sweden for a few days. The familiar blackbird wakes me, the pull of the call of passing geese. Blue sky, crows, clouds, thin and windswept like the American President's hair. The moon is a white crescent. I yearn for the allotment, to see the baby beans. It is still only early spring in Sweden: apple blossom budding, cascades of spring bulbs, wild lilies breaking through grass pathways in the botanical gardens, peonies weeks away. Light, though, is there before 4 a.m., still insistent after 10 p.m. The ground cold for growing.

The London sun's up by 5.30 a.m., catching alliums on the kitchen table. London is lit and quiet, nothing much stirring except me and the birds. There is a delicious melancholy sometimes in being awake on your own, moving almost silently, slowly, your thoughts louder in the ether. Feelings unrequited.

May 22

4.33 a.m.

The sky streaked dusty pink. The moon hangs barely there like a balloon caught in firelight as it passes. My heart lifts when I wake, like seeing an old friend. There is a comfort in walking around in soft light, an accepting quiet place for thoughts. I have missed these moments, the call of the moon, an allure like a souk stall, perfumed, kohled eyes calling. Join me, it says, move and think and feel freely, unencumbered by the day and life.

For me at least there is poetry here, a quiet rhythm to the day I can hear. A sun salutation. I was at the allotment late, stirring horn manure, a biodynamic dusk preparation, the sister light to this, a slight sigh, a release, an exhale. The earth is warmer now, the day's light longer, the sowing eager to grow. The same energy is here in dawn. An urgency, joyful, the romance of the day, a siren singing, as though you may have lost the ability to need only air to breathe, developed gills, swimming in different waters, free to float, drift, wash up on wilder shores.

My morning: Benjamin Raynard

First, could you tell me a little about yourself?
My name is Benjamin Raynard. I am forty-seven and run a small mail-order flower seed business from my narrowboat, *Casper*.

What time do you wake up (and why)?
I wake up and get up at 4 a.m. Before I started to work for myself I used to loathe the mornings. The truth is, it wasn't the mornings I hated, it was my job. Mornings are powerhouses if you know how to work them. The stillness of the pre-dawn hours have a subtle playfulness about them. Non-morning people might roll their eyes if you use words like sacred or magical to describe this time of day, but it is sacred ... and magical.

Do you have a morning ritual?
My morning ritual is very dependent on the season. Right now it is mid-winter. I wake up naturally at around 4 a.m., I clamber over my bedfellow, a fourteen-month-old Hungarian hunting hound named Flash. The first thing is to boil water for coffee. While that is on the gas burner I will attend to the multifuel stove. Presently the boat is icebound, the canal is frozen. Keeping the boat warm is paramount. The embers will still have a glow from having been banked up the previous evening before I turned in. I count out twenty-four pieces of coal and put them in the fire. This sounds like I may have a disorder but in fact it's a system that works. Twenty-four pieces of coal every eight

hours keeps the boat pleasingly warm without getting too hot. I sleep in the main cabin and leave the fore cabin as a seed store because it can be sealed off and kept cold and dark, perfect for flower seeds.

The bed in the main cabin needs to be folded back to a single bunk during the day. I do this while the kettle is coming to the boil. When everything is ship-shape, I sit down in front of the now roaring fire and have my first coffee. Until 5 a.m. I do very little other than get warm and let the coffee wriggle itself into my brain. At 5 a.m. I get to my desk and go about whatever task it might be for the morning. Perhaps writing, perhaps packing up orders. I keep my head down until 7 a.m. I probably get half of my day's workload done in just these two hours.

This time of year, at 7 a.m. dawn is just starting to creep up. Flash will suddenly sit bolt upright like he has been summoned by the sun itself and it's time for us both to go out. I usually have my boat moored up rurally. If Flash doesn't get a good five-mile walk in the morning he will come back and try to eat the boat. We are generally out for about an hour and a half, after which we will breakfast and take a well-earned nap.

How does being awake early affect your life?
Understanding how the early hours of the day can be so productive has utterly been life-changing for me. It has allowed my business to prosper, the consequence of which means that I have been able to offer myself time to do the things I want to do with my day.

What time do you sleep?
From 9 p.m. to 4 a.m., with one or two catnaps during the day.

Does your sleep vary through the year?
My sleep pattern doesn't seem to change.

Is the light important?
Watching dawn unfold on our morning walk is a great way to start the day. But for me, it's the two hours before dawn that are the most precious. Before the dawn the hours are mine alone. From dawn the day is shared with everyone else.

What do you like least about being awake early?
If I go out with friends of an evening I am absolutely ready to fall asleep in the pub by 10 p.m.

What do you like best about being awake early?
I've already answered this, I think.

How would you sum up your thoughts on your morning in 100 words or less?
The early morning is my friend and ally. If different times of the day were women, it would be pre-dawn to whom I would send flowers.

1 June	3 June	17 June	21 June
Sunrise 4.49 a.m.	*New moon*	*Full moon*	*Summer solstice*

JUNE

30 June
Sunrise 4.46 a.m.

June 1

4.50 a.m., Henne Strand, west coast of Denmark

Yesterday's gusts have largely broken overnight. The beach is easier to walk. The roses and grasses on the dunes echo with warblers. I follow the stream to the water's edge, white breakers running as far as I can see. The endless beach is empty except for me and a group of black-headed gulls surfing the wind without moving much. I gather empty razor clams and tiny cuttlefish skeletons like I used to feed my budgerigar. Yellow light over the river hugs the ground, the clouds are yet to break. The dunes here are huge, almost cliffs, mountainous. There are steep wooden steps for the more careful walkers. The sand line is punctuated by red-and-white sea rescue rings like from a beached ship. I walk, I muse, solitary, silent. A pair of swallows skim the dunes, follow its soft form. A small group wing-dance by the river, flutter and drink. The sky and the wild rugosa are more alive when I return.

June 2

4.50 a.m., summerhouse, Ahl Strand, Jutland

Darjeeling poured. A cycle ride to my favourite Danish field: a buttercup and wild orchid meadow with Icelandic horses and foals. Through banks of wild lilac, like a perfume trail. Skylarks are out in force though lower to ground than usual. The sun's just about breaking through. There is a summer soundtrack of larks, lapwings, woodpecker and the new cuckoo, the sound of long childhood summers. The foals are a little skittish as I crawl under the electric fence to lie and gaze at the marsh orchids.

June 3

4.10 a.m., post-dawn, pre-sunrise

Beach walking a few hundred yards past our summerhouse. A yacht has left the harbour, heading back to open water.

A small fishing boat bobs, anchored, in the bay. Opal light hangs in the east. I walk south along the water's edge towards the pink. A single gull rides the soft wind, an oystercatcher skims the waves, a duck, its flight slightly anxious as always (is it in the frenzied wings? I wonder). The sea is calmer than on the west coast. It is sheltered here. I walk past a mermaid made out of pebbles, shells for her tail, rose petals for her breasts.

The sky breaks towards the east where sunrise seems imminent. A pair of gulls call to each other as they too hug the water's edge. The swallows at first seem like a cloud of midges, scooting the sky in their hundreds, pairing off sometimes, mostly a liquid moving mass hunting high for the first sun rays. The walls of the sand cliffs have a stream of swallow holes at the top, where the roots of the wild roses are. A colony of summer. I watch, transfixed for a while. It's like they are dancing in the early light. The beach across the bay is lit by early sun.

I climb the path; the pennant pole and fir trees are orange-lit. The closed daisies will soon stir. The red rugosa, like so many blooded tissues (a TB ward?), brighten. I turn north, the sun on my right side, the sea on the other. More beach rock art: a shark, a wedding couple, prone on the ground, drowned or just resting. A pair of blackbirds scutter through seaweed, searching for a baby crab breakfast perhaps. A cat waits for movement on the path, slipping sullenly away as I approach.

June 16

3.03 a.m., Grebbestad, west coast of Sweden
I am meeting Göran Strömberg for *gökotta*, the rural Swedish tradition of a dawn walk maybe to hear the *göck* (Swedish for cuckoo). I am of course early, standing on the quay looking out over the bay: deep shimmering grey, metallic, broken by mooring poles and an occasional

red-painted fishing house across the water. There are dark clouds to the south, a rose-coloured patch on the north-western horizon, a fading ghost of last night's sunset. Warblers call from the beach rose, a subdued Swedish blackbird sounding thoughtful. *Gökotta* has almost died out even here, the ceremonial greeting of migrating birds, mostly on holy days: a celebration of the arrival of summer after long Swedish winter night. A week before the solstice, dark is elusive now, though the stillness holds.

We walk by the water, Göran carrying a bird book, one of many he owns, I am sure. Binoculars hang around his neck, a carrier bag with a hooded coat in his hand for the rain he says will come at 5 a.m. The rugosa share their fragrance as we pass. Foxgloves, trefoil, wild viola, yellow flag iris, flowering sea kale, all glimmer. There is driftwood washed up, sometimes elegantly twisted, salt-bleached trees beached among the seaweed. Remnants of when large boats would lie in harbour here while taking forest wood away. We climb rocks along the coastal path, past the fishermen's huts, over the bay.

The rain arrives on time, not good for cuckoo call but fine for whitethroat. I soak in the softness: dawn's greatest gift, the almost liquid air, the early day's slower, deeper breath. Sunrise's electric yellow-grey streams off steep hillside. There will be no *göck* today, just an occasional eider. We head back through insistent rain, take our *gökotta* picnic inside the oyster fisherman's house, door open to the sea. Last month's Danish cuckoo will likely be my last this year. Göran tells me 'cuckoo', sounding like the bird, is an old Swedish word for crazed. Maybe it is me.

June 21

0.58 a.m., summer solstice morning, Nordskot, northern Norway

The horizon here at the top of the world is crimson, lilac, violet hues, the sun mostly hidden. Unset. Unrisen. Clouds the colours of mulberry. An old mountain range still shows snow, all white only a month ago. This feels like a lost world, there could be dinosaurs. Cumulus like crushed velvet. Seas in shades of silver, old gold, mercury, shimmer under patches of broken sky, the sun barely contained. Caged by cloud, like embers of a dying fire. Bog cotton waves, white-haired like Einstein. Pools reflect, gulls swoon, soar, call, a small sound for a big bird. The mountains almost sullen, waves break on granite rocks like old land. Everywhere an ecosystem seeming in harmony. Small flowers making room for each other, none dominant: pinks, dogwood, yellow rattle, butterwort – common here as a summer culture for milk. Clouds blanket the peaks, the sun level with the break.

Can sunrise be the same time as sunset as the weather sites say? Where is dawn in near infinite light? Is it existential, a philosophical concept, perhaps an idea? Is there dawn chorus in a twenty-four-hour day? The mountains mock me in this land of impatient old gods, lords of a harsher life. The sun breaks through, a scant shred of sky, warms and lights the rock. Almost true north at midnight, now a torch beam on sea. Clouds darken, the breaks a more brilliant blue. My whisky glass is empty, the tufts of cotton grass glow, cloudberries form. The lighthouse is alight, a butterfly flies, maybe a moth.

Just past 2 a.m. the hedge birds sing, a dawn chorus with a less obvious dawn, though it's more obviously morning than minutes ago. The light's more apparently lifted. I wonder whether the timing of the bird call is guided by the positioning of the sun, polarising rays almost invisibly moving east now like the guidance system for migration. Dew forms, too. Is this because of a cooler temperature, though the sun has been 'rising' for two hours or at least moving east? Sunlight beams back from mountains though it is still subdued by cloud. I sleep, I wake before 5 a.m. I walk in light.

June 30
3.50 a.m., Royal Free Hospital, London, 12th floor
Windows locked. Blinds open. I stir, post-op, after three hours' sleep, sore and stoned on sorrow and oxycontin. Gentle light settles over London. I wish I could open a window, hear the birds below not the thrumming of a hospital, the quiet voices in the corridor. I am anxious to be elsewhere.

My morning: Philip Hoare

First, could you tell me a little about yourself?
I'm a writer, aged fifty-nine, living on the eastern side of
Southampton Water. I've published eight books.

What time do you wake up (and why)?
It depends on two cycles: the sun and the moon; the former
for the light and the latter for the tides. But where they
contradict, the latter wins out. This morning I woke at
3 a.m. because the full, pale green moon was shining
through my window and summoning me to the sea.

Do you have a morning ritual?
Yes. Wake. Water. Pray. Sea. Work. These change
if I am away from home, but they do so as little as
possible.

How does being awake early affect your life?
I've sometimes done all my work by 7 a.m. In a former life,
that would have left plenty of time to get drunk or take
drugs. But now I meet myself coming back – at 3 a.m. or
4 a.m., rolling back from Taboo or Heaven; now I'm cycling
to the beach. I see my younger self in the dark as we pass;
but, like the ferries I watch sailing up and down the Solent,
we never meet. But we still wear the same clothes. Except
for the bondage trousers. They're difficult to cycle in. Also, it
accentuates my antisocial nature, which is not innate. So it
is a retreat from human life, which is not good in one way,
but wonderful in another. Swimming is the most intimate

thing I do – I like to be accompanied only by very good friends, or dogs. Sometimes, whales.

What time do you sleep?
Eight o'clock, sometimes 7.30 p.m., till 3 a.m. or 4 a.m. In the hibernal season, a little later, maybe 5 a.m. if the tide isn't high. It is hard in midsummer to draw the curtains in my box bedroom. I feel like Ishmael or David Copperfield, banished to bed for misbehaviour.

Does your sleep vary through the year?
As above. I sleep a little longer in winter – cooler, darker, quieter. Sometimes the cats fighting or foxes howling wake me. Once I heard an appalling noise. It turned out to be two hedgehogs fucking under my window. Maybe it was the prickles.

Has your sleep pattern changed?
When I was a teenager, to get up to do my paper round, lugging a canvas bag full of the *Sun* and the *Daily Mail* around the suburbs on my bike was not an enticing reason to rise. Now the moment of getting up (not necessarily the moment of waking) is the best, least thought-polluted time of the day. Additionally, cold water – a snowy beach in February at 4 a.m. – is a wonderful way to reboot the brain. It is a little death. If most people die in the early hours, perhaps it is a good idea to circumvent the creator's designs and challenge your own mortality at that hour. Nothing else you do that day is as ecstatic or as stupid as standing, shivering on a sea wall, looking up at the moon in the hour between the wolf and the dog, or the pink and blue sky as the unseen sun lightens it. You hold that experience, that solitariness in the dark, that leaving of the land and your bed for the chilly quilt of the sea – you hold that secretly in your head and your muscles once they have stopped shaking.

Is the light important?
People think starlit night is brighter, but here a cloudy sky
bounces the light from the nearby port. I like that I
sometimes can't see where I'm going. My bike knows the
route so well – from road to trees to shingle – that it almost
takes me there on autopilot. The same with the water. This
morning, in the short hot darkness of a July night, the full
moon divided the sea in silver, and, in the distance, the
oil refinery was burning off excess gas, flaring in the
black water.

What do you like least about being awake early?
Nothing really. Sometimes I think too much, in the empty
space.

What do you like best about being awake early?
The empty space. The animals. The other day I heard
footsteps in the dark on the beach. I thought I'd been
rumbled. It turned out to be a fox, a vixen I think, coming to
check me out. We looked at each other, surprised at the
other being there. She didn't move. So I said, 'I'm just going
for a swim.' When I came back, she was still standing there.
Like a loyal dog.

*How would you sum up your thoughts on your mornings in
100 words or less?*
Monastic, indulgent, solipsistic, stupid, sacred, creative,
naked, exciting, hungry, cold, juvenile, irresponsible,
sensual, obsessive.

1 July	2 July	16 July	31 July
Sunrise 4.47 a.m.	*New moon*	*Full moon*	*Sunrise 5.22 a.m.*

JULY

July 6

3.14 a.m., London

Hot night, now a cool breeze. Quiet, an occasional siren. Gulls chatter, seemingly immune to night. There is blue-white on the horizon, east-north-east. First call comes at 4.04 a.m., a blackbird of course, quickly answered by crows. The horizon roses. The call increases in volume but is still almost thoughtful, quiet, not wanting others to wake, considerate almost. No longer the greedy, needy show-off sound of a male looking to mate. This is more a murmur. Dutiful. Beautiful. Gulls are calling louder, dark laughter as they fly by, contemptuous of those asleep. A young child's nightmare scream, a premonition perhaps. It is answered by a fox cough, like an old man clearing his throat. A harsher call of the four-legged wild. The sound of a lorry. The first person passing by, walking their scooter like a shopping trolley. There is a new and noisy fox family in the churchyard. I look out of the window in time to see them run free down the street.

July 12

4.14 a.m.

A night disturbed by incessant, insistent rain, knocking on the windows, dripping by the doors. All are wide open still because the cool the clouds bring is not enough and anyway the wind is from the north. The light is lower though how much is hard to tell from cloud cover. The hidden sunrise is later now, an inexorable minute a day. It will pass 5 a.m. this week, where it hasn't been since May. Rain signalling autumn although the signs have been here for a while: the allotment's dew, the browning of summer's green, flapping pigeons swarming the elder.

July 21

4.27 a.m., Corsica

Sitting on the beach looking south. Dawn here starts around now, where the deeper greyer-greens become more Mediterranean. The waves wash through and over sand. Every now and then an extra swell and white water rushes the rocks. Half the featureless sea and sky view is coloured cooler. The horizon slowly sketches itself as though by Hokusai. A darker, wetter streak in a watercolour world. Mist is promised. It likely won't last. It takes near half an hour for ripples to really show. The sky perhaps pinks a little, the blue-green settles longer on the cooler sea. Just me and the morning in deep Tibetan tones. I breathe with the waves. In. And out. The sun rises behind me around 6 a.m. Mist muddies the mountain outlines, smooths and softens (that word again) the lines, and the lights from the town across the coast. All as though painted by an Impressionist.

I walk along to another bay. Doves call like posher pigeons. My legs feel light. It's a smaller cove. A group of teenage kids under a tortoise shell of beach umbrellas have slept (a little) on the beach. They wake one by one with day. They look a little sheepish, as though amazed at their audacity. The first boy and girl pair off and head home. Their night too is over. By 6.30 a.m. I am back in the hotel room, the sky and sea, sister shades of opal, aquamarine, sapphire, precious stones.

July 26

4.03 a.m., London

Woken by the gentle percussion of rain on the roof terrace. The French doors half open. It rained on St Swithin's, will it be true for forty days? Otherwise the city is (almost) silent apart from occasional tyres on wet road. Back at my morning desk. Drinking cooling tea. Autumn has happened in the week I was away. No longer whispering, there are fallen conkers at the plot. The sky streaks grey. The first birds are gulls at 4.44 a.m., no musical chorus now. The blackbird is busy or subdued by the rain. His companions also keeping quiet. He finally breaks cover at 5.30 a.m., more a chatter than a sing-song. He makes more effort later but it feels as though it's almost over for him.

July 30
4.33 a.m.
Dawn after a night of torrential rain, rooftop doors mostly closed to protect the good rug. My sleep disturbed by splashing on stone tiles, a constant dripping. A jug of calendula, likely the last from the plot this year, is lit by the monitor, oranges and yellows, gathered yesterday, early morning, everywhere wet with dew. The leaves in the trees around me rustle, the green almost gone. A grey day is breaking on the horizon. A moody pink in the lower sky. The blackbird at 5.15 a.m., less a song than a nag, maybe a warning, not much musicality. By 5.29 a.m. a sweeter sound, a smaller bird, a tuneful whistle. The clouds have speeded, scuttling across the sky. I think about my brother and the first flowers we grew as infants. Christopher's calendula keep his memory alive.

My morning: Anna Koska

First, could you tell me a little about yourself?
I'm fifty, a mum to three, an illustrator and a beekeeper,
living in a field edged by woodland and water.

What time do you wake up (and why)?
I wake usually just before 6 a.m., sometimes earlier
depending on if the window's wide open to morning song.
The amount of light leaking through also plays a big part.

Do you have a morning ritual?
Many times it begins with lying still, eyes closed, trying to
work out how early it might be, trying to read the state of
the sky by determining the quality of light that has
managed to leak through my eyelids, and I'm listening to
the birds. Eventually I'll give in as the volume of the choir
increases. If it's a school morning, I'll make my way into the
children's rooms and wake them as kindly as is possible.
Hate doing this. If not, it's a case of creeping downstairs,
sliding the kettle over, and taking a mug of black tea out
into the garden. In the summertime my mug and I will
head out on a wet-leg walk through the field. This can take
ten minutes, or it can take an hour, depending on what
catches my eye. I'll take a photo of the morning, maybe post
it on Instagram.

How does being awake early affect your life?
It gives me some space in the day that would otherwise be
filled with must-dos and deadlines. It's only in the past

decade that I've come to appreciate this little window in time. I now cherish it, guard it as my own. It's at this moment when all seems possible, new ideas emerge and, although I'm not a writer, I often find myself sitting hunched at a computer, fingers galloping, tapping out an overflow of stuff that doesn't usually surface during the day.

What time do you sleep?
I'd love it to be before 10 p.m., but there's always something to pull the attention back from the stairs. It usually ends up being about 11.30 p.m.

Does your sleep vary through the year?
In the winter the birds begin later and the sun takes a while longer to emerge. There's less to disturb me, so my sleep is deeper.

Has your sleep pattern changed?
Having children has made me more sensitive to any click, cry or creak. I find it difficult to tune out, and so will often be roused by a ticking radiator or a fox shrieking in the woods.

Is the light important?
Yes, but less so the quantity. I love the seeping of light into shadow, find it joyful, the sun heaving herself up above the toothy jawline of old pines at the edge of the field. But equally so, to wake in the dark – perhaps with half an hour before sunrise – gives me a sense of being granted more of the magic than I was originally allotted.

What do you like least about being awake early?
The slouching dip in energy and concentration that usually spikes around 2 p.m.

What do you like best about being awake early?
Undisturbed and free thought.

How would you sum up your thoughts on your mornings in 100 words or less?
It feels like a gift; it just took me a while to realise. There's a lightness of thought that feels untethered from the body, yet absolutely yanks at the soul to come fly. I'd be awful at sharing it.

1 August	15 August	30 August	31 August
New moon	*Full moon*	*New moon*	*Sunrise 6.10 a.m.*
Sunrise 5.23 a.m.			

AUGUST

August 10

5.48 a.m., London

Feeling groggy as though overslept. There has been almost continuous rain for twenty-four hours. The temperature's rapidly dropped. I overheard a conversation at the bus stop yesterday, two old men on the death of summer, and it's hard to much disagree. Days are darker, wetter, there is heavy dew if no rain. Sunrise and sunset are so much slower. I feel drugged by almost eight hours' sleep. Dazed, a little dopy. The church foxes have been vocal through the night. Crows call, an occasional gull, but there is no early chirrup from the trees anymore. They have better things to do. The wind rips through rusting leaves. They are not far from falling. The year's fast falling, too. Fat layers of clouds move as sluggishly as me. The slow rising light feels more reluctant, almost invalid. My yoga almost matches the mood. I fight an urge to put on heating; I may be content with an extra layer.

August 15

3.40 a.m.

Up for dawn mangala-arati at Soho's Radha Krishna temple. It is Janmashtami, Krishna's birthday, a day of Hindu celebration. Excited young girls run around dressed in their best. A slightly bored bigger brother sits. Their preoccupied mothers talk together. Head-shaved devotees come down from the ashram upstairs. The air is quietly alive with excitement. Inside the temple room, a low drone of chanting, sitting people with their personal connection, a murmur of mantras. The room fills, an occasional devotee is pacing.

A lone singer calls the first chant, the room answers, a small finger cymbal shrills. The altar curtains part, revealing the Radha and Krishna deities. The chanting becomes louder, more fervent, a drum beats a tabla rhythm. The devotees and I swing slightly. There is an air of reverie. On the other side of the room, women cradle young children. The small girls follow the dancing of the female devotees at the front. The room has been decorated for the birthday celebrations, the ceiling garlanded in flowers and jewels, the deities specially dressed. It's the early start of a special day. The maha mantra calls: Hare Krishna, Hare Krishna ... ashram devotees to the front, householders at the back.

The swinging turns into shuffling. The frequency increases. There is rapture in the calling. Flames and flowers from the altar are passed around, smoke shared, water is sprayed. The room speeds up, the rocking movements coordinated and turning, almost like line dancing, arms are uplifted. There is ecstasy. The singing is excited. The room moves, feels alive, the calling confident. Respect is called for gods and gurus. It is an enlightened start to the day. The curtains close. The dancers divide into two rings, male and female at opposite ends. We circle a tree, significant though I don't know why.

As the pace and fervour build, I step out of the circle. The ecstasy is unfamiliar, perhaps akin to Dervish whirling. An occasional devotee glances over as they pass. There is compassion, care. After the mantras, we sit on mats for a reading. Plans and schedule are read out for the day. There will be fasting, midnight darshan, new dressing for the deities.

I find my shoes in the low light outside, walk out into Soho. It's still not 5.30 a.m. I pass another shuffling stranger, muttering to himself, though this time I see no connection, his reverie offering less release, his arm-waving less ecstatic. I grab an early bus, home before 6 a.m. A lone starling whistles, a melancholic call of migration.

August 19

5.45 a.m., West Sussex

Slightly fitful sleep, strange bed, strong drink. My sleepy wife waves to the sky, tells me I would hate to miss the sunrise. She turns over and returns to sleep. I dress in my pyjamas (it's my son's house in the country and best to walk around with clothes). There is a warming pink gathering behind the trees to the south of the garden. I make tea: the same kettle, the same Earl Grey as at home. I slip on a pair of his shoes, pad about outside in heavy dew.

It is a large formal garden, topiary, meadow at the bottom, trees with a swing, multiple inviting sheds, a greenhouse, a vegetable patch. I photograph fading, falling late summer daisies. I smell a heavily scented crimson rose. The sky is blue. The grass is wet. It is not cold. The tops of trees are soon crowned with sun. You can almost feel the warmth. A cock crows close by. The full farmyard call. Beyond the hedge a pheasant coughs. My book and the table turn yellow as the sun breaks over the low trees.

August 29

5.09 a.m., Denmark

Back in the summerhouse for the last gasp of summer. The deck is slicked with wet, the windows steamed. Drops fall from leaf to leaf, travelling down the tree; roof rain patters too, a slow and steady beat, marking morning time. Still almost dark, a greying sky, black wooden house, summer trees stand out against the waking sky. Tea made. A jug of late summer meadow flowers on the kitchen table softly stark. So quiet. Light breeze, a spider silhouetted (there are lots now, wrapping wooden doorways, laying traps from rose to roof). The sea rumbles in the distance, trees' autumnal rustle, a crow blows by.

The plot shrugs off night, changes into its morning coat. A slight chill talks of the end of August. Thin grey clouds pass by unconcerned, some kind of gull passes by. More calls. No hedge birds. The larch lightens, its spikes show. Silver birches sway. The first small call at 5.47 a.m., slightly anxious, solitary. A few rusty oak leaves are scattered through the deck. There may be blue. A pigeon calls, insistent, alone.

I wrap and walk to the beach, startle a fat frog in the covered path. It shuffles to the side, makes away slowly. A hare is in the clearing; its ears jump. It watches me carefully. I don't move. It returns to its dandelion breakfast. After a few minutes enrapt, I creep closer but the spell is broken, the hare runs, swerves onto the road, follows the curve. The sun is rising behind me, the far coast view is closer. It's Nordic clear, sky blue; seeeweedy clouds blown by the north wind. I wander down to the swallow cliffs, intrigued why stragglers are still swooping over the wheat fields. Gulls follow the coastline. The swallows' hole homes are empty, just me and the sea until I am joined by Danish skinny dippers.

A young couple wrapped in big beach towels, in and out of the water fast, they sit in the sun. A neighbour is here most days, long grey hair, drooping belly and moustache, he walks in and settles into the waves. Sunlight shines off silvered wet sea grass. As I leave, the doctor and his wife arrive in dressing gowns on bikes; they will be wearing costumes. Back home the house still sleeps.

My morning: Ian McMillan

First, could you tell me a little about yourself?
My name's Ian McMillan; I'm a writer and broadcaster;
I was born in 1956 and I've lived in the same village near
Barnsley all my life.

What time do you wake up (and why)?
Most mornings I wake up about 4 a.m.; I'm not sure why.
Sometimes the bloke next door goes out to work at that
time or comes in at that time. Years ago a lot of people
round here used to work at the pit and there were lots of
car doors slamming at this time. My dad was in the navy for
years and was often on the four-hour watch, so he always
used to wake up four hours after he'd gone to bed, so
maybe I've inherited that.

Do you have a morning ritual?
I wake up and lie listening to Radio 3 for a while. About
5. a.m. I go downstairs as quietly as I can. I do some press-
ups and some sit-ups and I lift some weights. I tweet some
ideas. I go for my early stroll at about 5.50 a.m. and when I
get home about 6.40 a.m. I tweet about what I've seen.

How does being awake early affect your life?
I feel fantastic in the mornings but start to fade away in the
afternoon. I'm sure it makes me insufferably smug.

What time do you sleep?
If I can, I go to bed about 9.30 p.m. and I sleep well.

Does your sleep vary through the year?
No, not really; winter or summer I wake up early.

Has your sleep pattern changed?
No, I've always woken up early.

Is the light important?
It doesn't really make a lot of difference.

What do you like least about being awake early?
I like it all apart from the fact I know I'm going to feel like death at about 4 p.m.

What do you like best about being awake early?
The feeling that I'm stealing something from the rest of the sluggish world.

How would you sum up your thoughts on your mornings in 100 words or less?
They are my diary, my almanac, my circle dance, my endless poem, my calendar, my memory bank, my myth kitty.

1 September	14 September	23 September	28 September
Sunrise 6.12 a.m.	*Full moon*	*Autumnal equinox*	*New moon*

30 September
Sunrise 6.58 a.m.

SEPTEMBER

September 2

4.15 a.m.

Editing, focused, clear of news, social media, other interference. Next time I look up it's 6.02 a.m. by the cooker clock. The first church bells are ringing in the distance. The priory blackbird's back, the garden is humming, the new cats are argumentative. The sky is sci-fi: primary colours fading to a gentler pastel wash. It is the first days of autumn, officially, though it feels summery. I have missed the first bus. I had planned to greet the light at the allotment. So instead I will look out at my daughter's garden, four doors away, sown for her May birthday; her pale sunflowers glimmer, sunrise soon.

September 15

5.35 a.m., Fern Verrow farm, Hereford

It is dark but a different dark to earlier. It is quiet but a different quiet, too. The room smells of sweet peas from the large bunch by my bed. The open window's gleam less grey than the room, framed by the pulled-back curtains. Rustling trees are faded black on black. I wash and dress by the light of the phone, moving as quietly as I can. I make tea in the dark of the kitchen. The kettle takes a few moments to find. I fill the pot by sound as always, a comforting familiar thought. The tea too I have brought with me; I carry it like my lucky beans. Some things it's good to always have around.

A dog rustles in the dark, paws scratch on stone floor, a nose presses into my side. We both want to go out. Lettice is a lurcher, not much more than a puppy, impatient, loving, curious. I search with fingers for my coat and boots by the front door; memory plays its part. It is cooler here by the black hills. Sunrise in the west by the Welsh border is ten minutes later than London, nudging towards 7 a.m. Then we are in the yard, dawn treading, with Lettice leading the way. I had thought to climb the hill out the back to get a better view, but she has other plans (I'd hate to lose her, she'll run faster than me).

I follow her shadow shape into the flower field. I haven't been here for years but it feels familiar. Tall pale anemones pick out of the gloom. There is a dull orange on the eastern horizon. Lettice scats about. I smell flowers. There are roses, lupins, chrysanthemums, sweet peas, cream-coloured nasturtiums. It is easier to make out the heads of pale flowers, the corn and dill silhouetted by the sky. I wander. Lettice loops. Saffron dahlias stand out. Ghost flowers. Lettice leaves. I am a little anxious in case I lose her. Moments past sunrise, there is a faint mizzle in the air. Time soon for breakfast, time to locate a misplaced dog.

September 20
6.03 a.m., London
Working, skyline warming, scattered cloud, cat calling wild. A knock on the ceiling. Henri can't sleep. A good eight hours is more important to her than to me. I snuggle in beside her, spoon warmth and even breath. It's the thing that works, that and sometimes another duvet. I bite down on my left index finger. It's what I do when I find it difficult to sleep (it doesn't happen often). I used to think it a breastfeeding thing, now I understand it is comfort in my own connection. I hold her, spread calming heat. I fall asleep while my wife stays awake.

September 22
5.12 a.m., Lapland, Sweden
It is the time of the autumn equinox, mid-heaven sun, equal day and night, though here in the far north they are fast losing daylight, day by day. By early December, sunrise and -set will be separated by mere minutes before there's no rise at all in the land of midnight sun. Smothering cloud

is barrelling up from the south so I use the phone compass to track north and east. I am out on a Torne River jetty by the Ice Hotel. Tonight I sleep at minus five surrounded by ice sculpture, but I wanted a warm room for this morning.

I am prepared. I have a Thermos of English tea and a Swedish cinnamon bun. I am wrapped up and wearing my new woollen hat. I am happy. I lie looking up. The jetty's holding chains moan. The river is strong, dark, powerful. Later, the clouds appear almost touched by pink and purple, but that may just be me. Light is coming reluctantly, only my compass telling me where the sun should be. Across the river, huskies howl, snow will be here soon and will stay until May. The river will deep-freeze. Birds, like people here, are few and far between, an occasional crow, a raucous cackle of magpies. Gold and copper rowan and birch across the water lift out of the gloom. The fir-treed crest of the low hills is spiked with treetops. The river darkens as the sky slowly lights, almost the only colour comes from dying leaves on deciduous trees. Here it is stark, austere, magnificent.

I sit on the jetty's edge, booted feet a couple of inches above the water, sometimes less. The forecast says the sky could clear for the first time in twelve days. There may be northern lights. I will be crossing the Torne by small boat later for a dinner of its fish. For now, in the far north, a warm breakfast calls then a bike ride to an old Sami church along the river bank.

My morning: Marlena Spieler

First, could you tell me a little about yourself?
Cookbook author, based in the UK for thirty years. Seven
years ago I was hit by a speeding SUV, and as a result lost
my sense of taste and smell. I have been working since,
as my senses healed, to relearn how to taste.

What time do you wake up (and why)?
I always used to wake just before dawn, regardless of the
season and time of sunrise. I have always awoken in a
cheerful mood. After my accident, it became different in
that I suddenly hated the early morning, and was unable
to force myself up and out of bed. The sunrise was part of
my pain; I couldn't even bear thinking about it. I'm
re-establishing my relationship with the early
morning now.

Do you have a morning ritual?
Coffee, coffee, coffee. Sometimes tea. With my hot drink,
and sometimes breakfast, sitting in front of a big window
and watching dawn transform the world. Once the daylight
has broken, I bring my husband a coffee. In summer I water
the garden, check my cucumbers, tomatoes, shiso, curse the
snails and slugs. In winter I might go back to bed, return to
the radio (and husband). Lately around dawn he brings me
a tea; THEN I get up like I used to.

How does being awake early affect your life?
When I was a single parent, it was a wonderful quiet time away from the pressures of everything. Later, when they were teens, my daughter and stepdaughter would get annoyed that I was perky in the morning. Now I would say the only way I am affected is that I get tired in the afternoon/evening. In the morning I'm energetic and bubbly; at night, cranky. Once I'm up, it's a race against time.

What time do you sleep?
Usually I turn the lights out by about 10.30 p.m. but sometimes it's a struggle to stay awake to even 9 p.m. When my husband is away (or I am) I sometimes like to cut myself off from any sort of schedule: going to sleep early or staying up late makes me feel as if I am two different people. Sometimes, as a special treat, around midnight I make a big bowl of spaghetti and crawl into bed with it.

Does your sleep vary through the year?
When I first moved to the UK, I was amazed at how late dawn arrived in the winter, and how early in the summer. I was from California, a more Mediterranean climate with less extremes of day/night length. Funnily, winter I could deal with, but summer was kind of wild. I always prefer to sleep with wide-open windows, feeling the air, aware of the dark, as well as stars, moon, streetlights … no closed curtains. But I was finding I couldn't go to sleep at night until the sun had set, and I was barely asleep before the world lit up again around 3.30 a.m. Now the UK feels normal.

Has your sleep pattern changed?
I have always loved waking up early. Then, seven years ago I was hit by a car and left with, among other things, two broken arms, an injured back and a head injury. My sleep

patterns were disturbed by the head injury. I became almost phobic of sleep, and terrified of the dawn. One of the most disturbing aspects of this whole thing is that when I would awaken just before dawn, as usual, I was reminded of how damaged and in pain I was, and I hated dawn, and I hated my life. I knew there was no guarantee that I would ever be OK again. Now, I can smell and taste intensely though erratically. I can write and think. I no longer feel terrified of the sunrise.

Is the light important?
The light is what I think about when I think about dawn, in summer when it might get all honeyed golden after sunrise, in winter when the dark night sky turns a pale blue-grey and lightens to a pale white-grey. In the winter it is the electric light, with its pale yellow glow, that I love best.

What do you like least about being awake early?
I hate being awoken by an alarm, and never use one. I tell myself I will wake up at a certain time and always do. Part of the joy of being awake early is moving at my own pace, an intimate time and space stretched out before me, quiet and without pressures.

What do you like best about being awake early?
I feel who I am most strongly at dawn. After my accident the dark turning to light terrified me. But as I've gotten better, being a part of dawn again is wonderful. And I do love early morning breakfast.

How would you sum up your thoughts on your mornings in 100 words or less?
Morning was taken away from me, then, eventually, returned. So, as hokey as it sounds, I do feel gratitude upon waking. Early morning, alone, is a little island in time:

neither night nor day, it's intimate. Cuddling my dogs, watching the quiet world, watering the garden, smelling coffee, eating breakfast, now I am doubly thankful: for the experience of the morning, each morning, and that I have been returned to myself.

1 October	13 October	28 October	31 October
Sunrise 7.00 a.m.	*Full moon*	*New moon*	*Sunrise 6.51 a.m.*

OCTOBER

October 1

4.05 a.m., London

Dark now, or as dark as the city gets with three-quarter moon, overcast autumn day. My mind is on my fathers and the allotment. It is Dudley Drabble's birthday, the foster father who took my brother and me in, gave me countryside and curlews, my love of early mornings. With him came safety. I was no longer sick. I would get up early and leave the house, wander through fields and lanes, along the river, let my imagination conjure ancient companions. For a while we boys felt loved, before his disappointment.

Ray Jenkins, too, is on my mind, another of my fathers. The one my children are named for. The man who adopted us as babies before soon handing us back. His funeral is this week and I am going to support my sister. There will be six of us. No flowers. His will says so. They weren't healthy or happy days with Ray and I have been waking between 2 a.m. and 3 a.m. this week, thinking fairytale thoughts, dosing myself with strong chamomile.

I sit, I wait, I read, I buy buns and bread when the bakery opens. It's the big allotment barbecue today and I will be manning the flames: cooking kebabs and sausages, heating vegetable stew. I sort through this year's seed, my brother's marigold like we grew with Dudley, as close as we had to a dad. Summer is (also) tired. It's over now. Time to pack it away.

October 6

Up again before 3 a.m.

Early even for me. My sleep has been disturbed, funeral looming, dark thoughts looping in the gloom. My rituals feel thinner, my safety net gapes. Venus is visible. The harvest moon is shining, the sky clear, air crisp. My window's open, my radiator on. A cat calls close to a howl, the birds are still asleep. Dawn rises around six, the light more obviously east. A helicopter grumbles, lingers overhead. Cops most likely looking. Sunrise is past 7 a.m. Soon the taxi will be outside, a short train trip to the past, back to being Peter for my patient sister. We will stand together, sing Christian songs. It will be over tomorrow. Almost.

October 8
4.20 a.m.
Liam is back from university and sleeping downstairs. We have been missing him like a cat with lost kittens, mewing in corners, calling his absence. I make tea and write and read as always. I think I can feel Ray's hold lessening, his bony grip less sure. Freedom from the wrong father. I have been sleeping four hours a night, more often less, since he died. I'd like the numbers up a bit. I work on writing, filing fears, packing up his lurid ghost.

Liam is returning to Leeds today so I want to cut him some allotment lunch. I am at the plot before sunrise. The giant amaranth is falling, the tagetes too. I gather nasturtiums for memories and colour. Autumn dew is pooling. I fill a bag with flowers and chard for a taste of home before he goes.

October 12
4.44 a.m.
The first blackbird calls, almost a whistled whisper. I have missed him, my once constant companion, near quiet for a while. The half-moon hangs high in the sky as though pinned. The lost cat is quiet. He has been howling for the past few days but it sounds like he found his way home. A neighbour's light goes out, the end of a long day. Mine beginning. The overnight rain's stopped, the air cool, the window open, the city as close as it gets to contemplative.

The church bells insist it's 5 a.m. Still no lights and not much movement except the blackbird, a little braver now. Sunrise is still two hours away; the clocks will soon be falling back. Winter will be here. Orange Mexican sunflowers from my daughter's garden smile in the screen light. The sun rises past 7 a.m., a red sky morning warning. Soundtrack: the church cross is now crowded with unsettled starlings.

October 15
5.45 a.m., Denmark
I light the fire by feel, find the smaller logs, the lighter, by fingers. It is darker here on the Jylland coast. I sit and watch the firelight build as the small flames lick at the logs. I empty yesterday's ashes, avoiding low branches. It takes time to adjust my sight outside. The sea rumbles through the woods. On the beach, a shadow: a running dog. There is no other human here. Then two sharp shots in quick succession over the bay. A life likely snuffed. Hunters waiting for deer at dawn.

The sky and sea seem stuck. Clouds to the east open like a shredded curtain. Silvered light breaks softly. There is a slow glow like a small fire thirty degrees north-east, the moon a Siva sliver. To my right, the day blues in broken shards, paler oranges, perhaps yellow. The stars shine, the moon breaks free, sits mid-heaven. The sky moves fluidly, an hour from sunrise. It's almost symphonic. The eastern orange embers. A dying firelight signalling the start of day.

By 7 a.m. the glow's gone, light's pouring through. The tree skyline sharpens. The first bird calls. The wind quickens. The cloud is muslin now. Sand and seaweed. Lacy waves break on the shore. White shells stand out. There is urgent song from the fir trees. I stumble over a gaggle of pheasants in the wheat field. There is a gathering of cranes. The peewits loop in murmuration. A goldcrest feeds on the oat sheaf in the garden. I smile at the sight of our tiniest bird.

October 19
4.10 a.m., Doncaster

Early breakfast at Howard's dad's. A pink grapefruit, halved and segmented, a special spoon; hot porridge, toast and tea. We have stopped for the night on our way to the Yorkshire Sculpture Park to see the James Turrell Deer Shelter at dawn. I have lately become obsessed with Turrell's work with light, particularly his Skyspaces, and have negotiated early entrance to the park. 'My work has no object, no image and no focus,' Turrell says. 'With no object, no image and no focus, what are you looking at? You are looking at you looking.' We arrive at the park two hours before sunrise, passing a flock of sheep I first think are perfect concrete sculptures, until they turn and move.

We are soon in the shelter. Imagine a Mayan temple rising out of an early Victorian brick building made to shelter park deer in winter: a pyramid nestled inside an arched structure with a skylight in the roof open to the elements. There is a matching square on the cold concrete floor caused by rain and other elements; leaves gather under walls. Lit low, the sides are neutral, the skylight stark and black. We settle on the warmed stone seating. We are wrapped up for the cold with chocolate, licorice and Howard's dad's Thermos. We stare at the sky. Occasionally, we step outside to compare light. 'The simple act of witnessing the sky from within a Turrell Skyspace,' his site says, 'notably at dawn and dusk, reveals how we internally create the colors we see and thus, our perceived reality.'

We are here to bear witness, create our own colours, test our realities. We lay mats on the floor in the middle of the square, revel in the Skyscape. The black becomes deep blue-black, the surrounding colours warm. The concrete floor seeps cold. The ceiling cream turns apricot as the framed sky lightens a little. It becomes 3D, perhaps filmic, not yet infinite. What was light becomes dark, what was dark becomes bright.

I step outside. The sky (of course?) is lighter still, dawn is coming pink. The outside arch frames the scene like a Renaissance painting. The trees layer. The hills start to show. Over the course of the next two hours the skylight radiates an intense azure like a Mediterranean door. An Yves Klein ultramarine comes alive. Crows call through the aperture. My camera cannot cope, compensating like my brain, but slower, for the light and colour from moments before. The framed colours only exist in the room, at best a distant cousin to the skyscape outside. Renaissance becomes Constable as the grass intensely greens. The sheep whiten. A Henry Moore bronze appears, its giant size dwarfed by landscape made more majestic. It's bucolic now, of course. An old ram trots to a passive ewe, his head dropped to nudge between her legs, as she resignedly makes room.

Inside, white clouds wash overhead, the ceiling browns to caramel. We watch transfixed. It is almost psychedelic. It's certainly sublime. Difficult to comprehend. Easy on the eye.

October 20

5.30 a.m., Mirfield, Yorkshire
It's morning in my monastic cell at the Community of the Resurrection. I have been put in contact with Prior Oswin by Christopher Irvine, canon of Canterbury Cathedral, who used to be based here. He has been explaining the liturgy of the hours. How the Christian monastic day starts with evensong, and the importance of compline (completion) service, quietness and reflection (Lord, now you let your

servant go in peace), through silence to matins and the resurrection. Morning service for the risen son.

Matins in this community means gathering for service at 6.45 a.m. Dawn at this time of year. I wash, dress, go outside and wander through the rose gardens. It is countryside dark, a little difficult to see, just garden ghost petals, a pallid, autumn luminescence. The eager motorway roars in the distance. Constant movement on the M1. No time there for contemplation. I walk, maybe feel, my way through the organic orchard. As I return to the building I find one of the old brethren at the door, unsteady, unsure on his feet. I hold it open for him. Another brother, on his way to morning service, arrives to turn on lights. He smiles at his companion, says quietly, 'All will be well.' Night-time silence is broken then gathers again. I want to believe him.

I am inside the church early and find a seat at the back. A couple of brothers sit in their inside semicircle, facing the altar. A bell tolls, solemn, slightly urgent, then again. Other brethren shuffle in, dressed in black and grey and sandals. It is austere here. The community is small, mostly elderly. There are just seventeen. They are not all here but some are joined for dawn by a couple of lay visitors and me. People come here for retreat. They are warmly welcomed. Morning prayer is sung sweetly by one strong clear voice, reading from a smartphone. Then the community follows. There is no accompaniment. Just the male voices of a monastic Christian choir. The canticles echo. The acoustics continue through the church. The morning light uplifts. There is blessing.

Afterwards, we gather for silent breakfast. Tea, fruit, porridge, like boarding school. There is honey and their home-made marmalade. Bread is broken.

October 21

6.35 a.m., Dartmouth, Devon

Back in my home county, near where I was born. There was a storm last night. Umbrellas were upended, broken-spined, discarded. The tide threatened. Dawn comes more peacefully. Outside, the yacht masts still rattle. Constant coastal noise. Curiously comforting. I draw back the nets. Pink hugs the hills over the river. Treelines silhouette like canine teeth. Pre-sunrise pewters on the river. The landscape rolls like only Devon. Car beams gather, signal impatience across the water. The ferry starts sluggishly. The town feels a little hungover. The food festival is in full swing. Tents and tarpaulin crowd the quay. I am being interviewed later about my river childhood close to here. There will be questions, readings, there may be tears.

October 28

6.10 a.m., London

The last day of summer time, sunrise 7.47 a.m. It will be December 4 before it is this late again. A last sunflower glows as I write. It is cut from Kala's garden, still coming strong, the nasturtium too. The sky streaks, the red crane tops glow around Canary Wharf. By 7 a.m. the elusive blackbird calls, almost reminiscent of spring. It is short-lived. A magpie crows. A door shuts. A top-floor light comes on. Henri has to leave early so no rushing to the allotment on the bus around the corner. For now, the sky glows quietly crimson, almost east, extinguished in a minute. Seagulls mourn the end of summer.

October 29

4.05 a.m.

GMT: the average moment the sun crosses the meridian and reaches its highest point in the sky. Today we rejoin. Return to Mean Time. Fall back. It is the first day. I wonder if I've gained an hour or misplaced it. It will be a little brighter a little earlier for a month, though I've never minded the darker mornings. For now the first bus is close to sunrise. A blackbird sings in the denuded maple. Funereal clouds cross the sky.

At the stop, scattered rice and flower petals mark different ways to do Saturday night. My three bus companions huddle down as though trying to hide. Their heads disappear. It is dark. The streets sulphurous. Ragged trees holding onto a handful of handkerchief leaves. Pilgrims Lane, the bus calls. It's just me and someone asleep. Past the bread-shop workers stacking shelves. A man with a woolly hat is shouting. Is it because his hat covers his ears? Yellow leaves float like butterflies.

It's still dawn at the allotment: 6.40 a.m. I arrive with light. I pick red shiso and nasturtium. Roses are dewed. Amaranth is over. I mooch. I commune. I soak it in. I pull up the sunflower skeletons, scatter their seed on the table for birds. I carry giant spines to the compost, saving a few flower heads for next year. I leave content, close to 8 a.m., a quiet day in store.

My morning: Lemn Sissay

First, could you tell me a little about yourself?
I'm a writer. I present BBC radio documentaries and occasionally present for television. I write plays and occasionally I write articles. I perform my poetry on stages throughout the world. I am an Ethiopian Briton born in Wigan who lives in London. I am Chancellor of the University of Manchester.

What time do you wake up (and why)?
I wake between five and seven. For as long as I can remember I have woken early. As a child I thought the world awoke as a theatrical production with me as the sole audience member. I thought everyone experienced this.

Do you have a morning ritual?
I write a morning tweet that describes how I feel and how the morning is to me at that point. The only criterion is that it has to be original. The words have to never have been written before ... since the beginning of time. This takes between thirty minutes and three hours to create. This morning it is:

> I am not defined by darkness
> Confided the night
> At dawn I am reminded
> I am defined by light.

How does being awake early affect your life?
I get more time in my day. It is a coincidence that this is the best time to appreciate nature. Nature talks to my inner world and early morning is a gift to that.

What time do you sleep?
I go to sleep between 11 p.m. and 1 a.m.

Does your sleep vary through the year?
In winter I have been known to sleep for longer. Especially when feeling depressed. Depression always came with the dark days. However, this stopped. So I am blessed with waking early in winter as much as summer now. I used to be able to count down to depression in early October and my good mood would return in April/May.

Has your sleep pattern changed?
Once I stopped drinking alcohol the pattern changed. The rhythm of depression in winter along with longer hours in bed stopped. I also stopped projecting my mood onto the weather. I now appreciate light for what it is rather than as an ego boost for my mood state.

Is the light important?
Oh, light is everything. It is my one reason for changing rooms in hotels. I spend half my life in hotels. Light and the appreciation of light has been one of the greatest gifts of my life. Light charges me. Light changes me. I know this is a contradiction to my last comment but it does. Sometimes in the street I tilt my head sideways so the sun can get on more of my face. It feels like being stroked on the cheek by a lover, a mother, a brother, a friend.

What do you like least about being awake early?
That other people are not awake early. Because meetings in the morning are fun.

What do you like best about being awake early?
That I catch the world napping. That thousands of people around the world now read my morning tweets. They are not guaranteed to be great works of art. And this inspires me to try my best. This is a real shot in the arm. It is the emotional and artistic equivalent of warm water with lemon. It starts my constitution for the day and sets the agenda. I feel my productivity in the morning is a gift. It means I can get things done. It means I begin the day connecting to what is important. Though I don't subscribe to religion it means that I can connect to a power greater than myself.

How would you sum up your thoughts on your mornings in 100 words or less?
In four lines.

> Stand up for light
> Stand down the dark
> Or sleepwalk into night
> With a shadow for a heart.

1 November	12 November	26 November	30 November
Sunrise 6.53 a.m.	*Full moon*	*New moon*	*Sunrise 7.41 a.m.*

NOVEMBER

November 2

5.05 a.m., Central London Mosque

A small group of bearded men huddle by a locked gate on the edge of Regent's Park. It is cool, dark, pre-dawn. I am here for Fajr, the first Islamic prayer of the day, beginning at *subh sadiq* – 'true dawn or the start of twilight when light first appears across the full sky' – and ending at sunrise. The imam I was to meet has been called away so I am attending my first Fajr solo. The gate is unlocked. I follow my companions across the court and into the domed prayer room. I find a central space close (but not too close) to the front and the devout. There are perhaps a dozen of us: Arabs, Bangladeshi, Somali, Sudanese mostly.

The air is solemn but welcoming. It isn't warm. Almost everyone keeps their coat on, one young man prays near a radiator. Some settle in chairs to read scriptures, most kneel. There is a large electric clock on the wall, signalling today's prayer times. These change depending on dawn. At 5.15 a.m. an electrified call signals the start. My companions mutter their personal prayers. More people arrive. There are quiet smiles and handshakes. The air is expectant. The room lines up. I stand in a second row, the gaps by my sides close. It is comforting.

An imam calls the prayer at 5.40 a.m. There are maybe a hundred of us now, shoulder to shoulder, stockinged feet to stockinged feet. I follow my companions' lead. We kneel, we pray, in unison, mostly strangers, gathered here by the park from around the Islamic world, in simple but solemn recognition that God is great. By 6 a.m. we gather our shoes and drift away to our days. The light is lifting. The sun is close to rising. *Allahu Akbar*.

November 5

4.50 a.m.

The full moon wakes me for the third time, bright like a torch beam through the trees. I can read the church clock now the leaf has thinned. I can be woken by moonlight. My daily dahlia companions are barely weekly. These were almost past their best when I bought them. It's been time for more chrysanthemums. The plot tagetes are exhausted, too, though I have saved big bags of seed. The sun when it comes is sharp and bright, the air crisp but with warmth. A heath walk calls. But first breakfast. Perhaps the shop for papers.

November 6

6.45 a.m., Hampstead Heath

Cold at three degrees. Crisp frost, the first of the year, has turned the long grass almost white, causing it to lie low as though exhausted. I am meeting David Darrell-Lambert, birdwatcher, at the top of Parliament Hill. He is there to track migration, make note of the species and numbers. It's the highest spot in London, a panorama of city sky. Mist sticks to the hollows, gathers on the water. It is almost sunrise. There is a soft orange to the horizon, you can see the city curve. The sky is clear, good for spotting movement.

Linnet! says David suddenly. He scans with his binoculars. I see nothing. Scope the small sound. Then there it is, tiny, at the top of the world. Chaffinches next, a group of eight swooping dots, piling out, David says, of colder northern Europe. For an hour we watch flocks and groups of birds, sometimes single, sometimes pairs, mostly flying high, intent on crossing the city. Too high to see markings. David relies on call and flight and thirty years of experience. He started as a young boy and has been deep-hooked since. He tells me about my tawny owl's winter call, the best spots and times and months for dawn chorus, which birds are active when. All the time tapping numbers into his phone.

It is exhilarating, his enthusiasm deeply infectious. I watch jackdaws, a greater woodpecker, rarer bramblings, redpolls, doves, hundreds of pigeons, speed across the sky, all heading in the same direction, south and west away from the north. To warmth and light, a better life. Refugees with wings.

November 9
6.50 a.m., Ballycotton, Ireland
Dawn in a coastal village. The sky is grey, the water deep green and flat as stone. I am in east Cork to meet Myrtle Allen, ninety-three-year-old pioneer of Irish cooking. But first a walk to the sea and to see the Ballycotton boats that supply her restaurant. A fisherman paddles a broken boat to his small scallop dredger in deeper water. They have all seen better days. Herring gulls scream and strut the harbour wall. I wander out on the cliff path towards Ballyandreen. Gorse and water to my left, iridescent fields to the right. The cloud in front lifts.

Sunrise here is 7.45 a.m., half an hour later than London. The north-east horizon glows. The bushes are alive with wrens and warblers, the fields dotted with curious cows. A young heifer gathers courage to walk towards me. She stops, starts, takes her time. The coming sun is threatening to break through; this is not a day to hurry. A cloud of kittiwakes bob in the water, winter-gathering now in numbers. Crows skim the cliffs, diving close. Sun as yellow as Irish butter beams. The small boat stops. The sea glows gold as a wedding ring. I glory in it. The heifer skits sideways, amazed at her audacity.

I soak in the honeyed gorse, the bracken, the bladderwort, the song, the sea. I stop by the stile. Download it all for later, absorb the astonishing greens, the blues, the stubbled cornfield, the sunrise. I turn back for breakfast: there's raw Jersey cream and Mrs Allen's porridge.

November 10
6.45 a.m., Shanagarry Strand, Ireland
Strand is the old name for beach, same as the Danish; were the Vikings here? The weather is murky, there are spots of rain on the windscreen. The long beach is gravelly, dark sand, no shells but a tide of uprooted seaweed. The waves are still, just a surface fluttering of breeze. I look out at the Ballycotton lighthouse, fully automated now. The sea's like fish skin. A weatherworn concrete jetty is facing east to Wales and dawn. The sky clears as the sun calls. There's a lemon cast to the sky. A bent woman with a headscarf and bright yellow jacket is leading a reluctant dog. Both are slow and long in the tooth. The sea ripples, the sun breaks and conjures a strip of warm colour. Seagulls startle. A seal bobs, curious, comes close in to the beach. I am transfixed. Windblasted sky trails lead east towards England; all roads, they say.

November 19
5.05 a.m., London
I sleep without clothes but slip pyjamas on to walk about and write. I am thankful for them this morning as I stand out on the terrace. It's a consecutive morning of astonishing stars. Sometimes harder to see in the city. The once-familiar patterns are there: the plough, the planets. The super-crisp air is clear, near freezing at two degrees. I stand longer than I planned. Better with scarf and socks. The early bird is back. A sweet song that doesn't last long. I love these November mornings, leaves twisting like prayer flags. Filigree horizon now, a delicacy to the sketchy trees, as though quickly drawn in pen and ink. Even the tithonia in Kala's garden have almost given up.

Dawn is coloured apricot, punctuated with ducks, wildfowl on the move, soaring city gulls and clustered pigeons. We are coming to the last of the yellowing leaves. There is a lightness to the cloud, palest rose like candyfloss. Steam is coming off the tower. Everyone's heating on. The blue sky pales, the planes streak like a child's scribble but all still silent until the blackbird gets a second wind.

November 26
5.28 a.m.
Reading quietly for a while then out for 6.30 a.m. Sunrise more than an hour away, sunset before 4 p.m. for the first time in a while. It's cold at two degrees, cars are frosted, coated, almost shiny. We are deep in the short days of winter sunlight. The first-bus drivers know me by now: one of the two or three early people on the route, the only one not going to work or heading home. The Hampstead bread van man is making his delivery. The high-street Christmas tree glitters moneyed colours. The Dickensian streetlights look picturesque as I climb the hill.

I'm here to say sorry for neglecting the allotment, leaving her alone. The fallen leaves are browned, curled crisp, the soil glistens. It is beautiful, of course. Many of the plots have been hibernated. Others are netted and caged. Our nasturtium towers, once proud with peas and beans, are defeated, just a few late flowers shining through. Once invaders, their leaves are lost. The tagetes, too, are reduced, their reds rusted. I pick dried heads for summer seed. The sorrel has been stripped to the spine by pigeons, most of the amaranth fallen. A robin visits, head cocked and curious, to investigate broken soil. There is a pink cast to the cloud. I fill my pockets with tagetes seed and say thank you. I walk towards home and the rising sun.

November 30

5.15 a.m.

Last day of autumn, scientists say, though it's been icy all week. Woken first before three by an almost full 'supermoon' blasting beams like a lighthouse on the horizon. Next, the insistent owl, calling before dawn like the ornithologist said. It seems I have no immunity to the sound, its ghostly, needy echo of my childhood. It's a call like no other, more alien somehow. No tune but a beauty to it. Come love me, live with me, it says in its minimalist way: the Björk of birdsong.

My morning: Liza Adamczewski

First, could you tell me a little about yourself?
My name is Liza Adamczewski. I'm a painter and sculptor.
I was born in Dublin; my mum was on the run from South
Africa after Sharpeville. We left for London when I was six
days old. So I was made in Africa, born in Ireland and raised
in the UK. I've never felt that rooted. I like to take part but I
also like to observe. I'm comfortable on the margins. I've
just moved to Pembrokeshire from the Suffolk coast. I came
for the coastal landscape and the hills, such primal beauty.

What time do you wake up (and why)?
I wake up three or four times a night, finally giving in and
getting up sometime between six and seven although I can
start the day at five if I'm excited about something in the
studio. I think my sleeplessness stems from when I was a
single mother: you are always on duty listening out for a
crying child in the night. My youngest was premature. He
needed feeding every hour; I didn't sleep for three months
properly. It changed my body clock for ever. He's a
quantum physicist now so it didn't do his brain any harm.

Do you have a morning ritual?
I have a night-time ritual rather than a morning one. I have
to do the *Guardian* crossword puzzle at the dot of twelve
then it's radio on and lights out. When I get up I just have a
hot drink. At the moment it's black coffee and then I go to
my studio. I have breakfast when I take my first break. In
the old days, I had to make sure the house was tidy or the

mess would call me and interrupt my train of thought. Now that I'm working in a building site I have learned to ignore everything but painting, it keeps me sane.

How does being awake early affect your life?
I love waking up early. I can get a day's work done before 12 p.m. and feel smugly pleased with myself. It allows me to fit in loads of other stuff, like restoring our farm that hasn't been touched for thirty years. We are developing butterfly habitat for rare species and have very rare fungus, too. If I didn't get up early the butterflies would cop it.

What time do you sleep?
I go to sleep before 12.30 a.m. unless I have a good book on, in which case the radio gets neglected. I do flag in the afternoon and have been known to drop off for a very deep sleep.

Does your sleep vary through the year?
Ask my mother. She could never get me out of bed for school. I was a dreadful truant. School was a prison sentence.

Is the light important?
Light is always important to a painter. It creeps through my eyelids. I never have curtains. In my last house on the east coast the sun would rise over the sea and I would watch it from my bed ... in summer this made for a very early start.

What do you like least about being awake early?
There is nothing much I don't like about being awake early.

What do you like best about being awake early?
One of the best things is the dawn chorus. I'm going to make a recording of it and have it played at my funeral. I stand outside on a clear morning and it's like I'm the only person listening.

How would you sum up your thoughts on your mornings in 100 words or less?
They set my day's course like the rudder of a boat. Every day seems to be a new adventure. I wake up and am amazed to find myself in this new place. I look around me and think, This life of mine, it's not too shabby, is it?

1 December	12 December	22 December	26 December
Sunrise 7.43 a.m.	*Full moon*	*Winter solstice*	*New moon*

31 December
Sunrise 8.06 a.m.

DECEMBER

Herdsman

Berenice's Hair

Coma Cluster

Arcturus

Denebola

Lion

Serpent
(Head)

Virgin

Spica

Cup

Scales

Crow

Scorpion

Water Snake

SE

SOUTH

December 1

5.12 a.m., London

First day of Advent. I light the candle; it's a Danish thing, candle lighting; numbers one up to twenty-four are marked out on the stem. A siren howls. Winter's here at two degrees; there were snowflakes yesterday. It's no longer possible to ignore the coming of Christmas. Night streets are bustling. It's sort of comforting in the cold. A damp chill breeze bites through the dawn window. I close it and shut out the sound of lorries driving faster on wetter roads, deliveries to make. By 6.30 a.m. it's open again, the room snug enough now to take it. No birds, just occasional planes flying in. Cranes twinkle like on a Christmas tree.

December 2

5.12 a.m., Thornbury Castle, Bristol

A four-poster bed in our sixteenth-century tower, pretty much pitch-dark but for the Severn Bridge suspension lights to the west and Wales. We're sleeping in the same room as Nigel Slater when he worked here in its pomp: £11 a week, he says. The loo is literally a throne. Light when it comes is slow, lazy, late, country misty from the turret. The view is gothic novel, the old cloisters falling down, the vineyard wrapped for winter. Huge trees broken down like the walls. There is an ancient church in the back garden, crows clustered, calling ancient enmity. I wait for the executioner's knock. Henri, far away on the quiet side of the giant bed, sleeps still. I watch the daylight lick the high ceiling.

December 5

4.05 a.m., London

False dawn. Almost daylight. At least like dusk. The December supermoon is shrouded. Covered in cloud it is as light as 4 p.m., bright enough to see downstairs. In an hour

it shines through broken sky, a dramatic backdrop for the
church: the cold moon as it was called in my childhood
almanac. Finally it is free, casting pale shadows, projecting
window images on the wall. Clear cold day breaks to the
east. The back garden blackbird preens on an old aerial. The
sky is splattered with birds. I recognise groups of finches by
flight pattern. Geese and ducks indelible as always.

December 9
7.02 a.m.
Late night. Late morning. I've overslept. Woken by gulls
calling. A meeting, almost a murmuration: I watch them
surfing the student housing tower, riding the heated air like
raptors. Everywhere is ice, cars glittering, roof tiles, too. The
sky is clear, the temperature zero. Near a hundred gulls,
large and small, joyously swirling in the soon-rising sun.
A once-coastal community chasing city thermals like a
trawler with fish.

December 12
5.35 a.m.
London's background hum, an occasional motorbike, car,
the thrum of a night bus. I sit with the same tea every day. I
work in in-flight pyjamas. I am comfortable. The window is
slightly open. Crows croak. Occasionally Kentish Town
sounds like woodland. Table flowers and fruit are barely lit
by the computer screen. A couple of apples in the half light,
scented narcissi in a jug. Outside warring cats growl. They
have unfinished business about who bosses the back
gardens.

The slightly acrid smell of Tibetan incense creeps up the
stairs. After the kettle, lighting them and the small candle
for the Siva deity is the first thing I do. I don't sit. I don't stay.
I don't meditate. I light the candle and incense and leave the
empty room. It is for the thought and the deity and not for

me. But lighting the candle and leaving it in its own light and smoke is an important part of my morning. I have been doing it for more than twenty years, the days I am here. Perhaps I used to plan, make notes, things to do or say. Now I have let that go. It is like flying a kite, catching the wind, letting the line rip when it happens. The happy moment in a soft consciousness.

There is a trill of a blackbird, still slightly subdued. Someone opens the throttle of their motorbike. A few hundred yards away another window shows light. The rest are dark. One door lit yellow. Another small bird wakes. The charging toothbrush quietly flashes. I miss having cats, they are more night-time than me, but I couldn't deal with the pain when they died. The south-east sky shows redder night. Dawn is gathering. I close the window; the temperature shows six degrees.

I light another tea candle, lay out a mat, do salutations where the sun will be. I stretch, I twist. I breathe, I am still. I run a bath, squeeze oranges; soon everyone will wake. Two geese fly by the kitchen window, necks pointing south.

Time to get dressed, near time to walk to work. Through the street market, keeping an eye out for mangoes. Through the park with the dog runners. Detour through the pastel-coloured crescent for my favourite late rose and along the canal. East into the sluggish sun.

December 18
6.05 a.m.
Christmas week, recovering from a big family thing, again sleeping more than eight hours. It is dark. A 'near new moon: 1 per cent waxing crescent', the almanac site says. Sunrise is now peaking past 8 a.m. and climbing till January 1, the turning point of the sun and the year. It won't be back in the sevens for a month. The winter solstice is three days

away. The world outside seems still. Gulls come with pale rose-petal dawn. A crowd calling my Devon childhood. The first songbird breaks night silence like a monk. *Take these broken wings and learn to fly ...*

December 20

3.05 a.m.

Restless. Christmas was long compromised for me. My first memories, mostly bad. And unsettling still, it seems. Awake before 3 a.m., at least an hour early. Thinking of my early disconnect from 'normal'. Of the strangers I shared my life with. The unexplained absences. I was too young to understand then. Too old now. My dead brother's birthday barely a week away. It is time for morning mourning. I surrender to sadness, slip out of bed, make chamomile tea, sit at my cool open window. I breathe deep, summon memories from dark.

And here he is: Christopher. I mostly think of him aged six or seven, while rescue was still possible. He has a cowboy hat, a cap gun, an excited smile. Just us and people we didn't know. We clung. I climbed him like a vine. We stuck. Happy Christmas was for others. Still is a little. Hence the chamomile. The tree is lit. A candle too. Like church. I am conflicted about faith. My gods have long been a more fluid thing. There in the sound of songbirds, the flash of a running hare, a fox passing a window. And, of course, in kindness. I return to bed to cuddle my wife and find my missing hour.

December 21

6.25 a.m., winter solstice

Out with the early cyclists, early walkers, people buying early papers. Across the road the Dominicans are calling morning prayer. I post the last of the Christmas cards in time for the first collection. All working-class workers on the bus to Hampstead, mostly women, mostly tired. Most get off at the hospital in time for the early shift. An old stray man with a stick gets on. Where do all the lonely all belong? I am armed with Danish Christmas beers, special brews to leave on other allotments. It is pre-dawn. The Victorian street lights look like a scene from *The Exorcist* but they are alive with early song.

The allotment site is dark: brooding trees, gloomy greening ponds. There is a light mizzle and tuneful chatter from the wood-bird community beyond. I pass by friends' plots, leave my Christmas cans. For John and Mary, Annie and Jeffrey, my growing companions. I place cakes, a gift and beer in the shed for Howard. I sit and soak it in: my special place on a special day, my plot of quiet and communing with birdsong and soil. The light lifts, the clouds stay. Me too. It is the last time I will be here this year. I say my silent thanks. I will be back soon in the New Year. It will already be a little lighter.

December 24

6.10 a.m., Danish coast

The quiet time before sunrise when the sea and owl call in winter, the cuckoo and songbirds in spring. It is when the world wakes and so can you. I do.

I light a fire, there is most of a moon and it is never as dark as you think. Electric light is for others and evening, though I will turn on the tree when the family wakes. The Christmas candle flickers, the hellebore (Christmas rose, they call it here) catches the glow. It's soon snug with crackling logs I split yesterday. This Danish thing called *hygge*. Sunrise is near to 9 a.m. There is time enough to snuggle down like dormice before I walk the beach at dawn.

Wrapped: jumper, fleece, windproof jacket, winter socks. The smoke smells almost kippered. The world is empty, just me and the south wind, an occasional white-headed wave, perhaps yellowing light to the east. I stand, I walk on sand, I wander in wonder.

A dove calls as I leave. It is time to refill the stove. Hedge birds are scurrying in the half light. I have hung feeders, scattered peanuts and sunflower seed. The bushes are alive with linnets, bramblings, scarlet bullfinch, goldfinch, hawfinch, an abundance of bird riches. Later a small family of pheasants will join them. Meanwhile, I watch and wait for others to stir. It is Christmas Eve, the big Danish day. More family are coming. There will be roast goose, red cabbage, rice and almond pudding; someone will win a marzipan pig.

My morning: Samuel West

First, could you tell me a little about yourself?
My name's Samuel West, I'm fifty-one years old. I'm an
actor and sometimes a director. I live in London with my
partner, the writer Laura Wade, and our two daughters.
One is three years old and the other was just born.

What time do you wake up (and why)?
I've always woken around six. When I was at school it was
to do last-minute homework. At university I didn't drink
coffee (or take any other stimulants, sadly) so I had essay
crises in the early morning rather than work into the night,
which has always been the sleepy end of the day for me.
Since becoming a father I get up early to get my first
daughter her milk and to dress her, and since discovering
the joys of birdwatching about twelve years ago, both
Laura and I have enjoyed an early morning start to our
days out birding.

Do you have a morning ritual?
The first thing I do on waking, I'm afraid, is to check
Twitter. I'd like to instigate a policy of no screens in the
bedroom, but I'm incapable of it at the moment. Recently,
during a decent period of unemployment (four months
plus), I started going to the gym for an hour before getting
our daughter up. Exercise makes me feel smug, and if I do it
any later in the day, I get less time to feel smug before I fall
asleep (also, I mostly don't go). So now four times a week I
get up, have coffee, toast with peanut butter and Marmite

and some creatine and head to the gym at 6.30 a.m. for an hour, then come back and make tea, milk and toast for the family.

How does being awake early affect your life?
On January 2 this year (January 1 was a complete washout), Laura and I, leaving the daughter with her grandmother, left the house at 5 a.m. and reached Lynford Arboretum, on the Norfolk/Suffolk border, ten minutes before sunrise. We're both pretty murderous that early in the day, and we have a playlist of soothing music for the car which stops us killing each other. It's often difficult to get to a wood by sun-up (and if you want to hear the dawn chorus, it can mean rising at 3 a.m. in spring), but I have never, ever, regretted it. The disadvantage is that by the other end of the day I'm drowsy and sloth-like. This is only really a problem when doing a play, and in that case I try to sleep in the middle of the day for a bit. Evenings out get rarer, but what with ticket prices and babysitting we can't afford too many of those anyway.

What time do you sleep?
Any time from 10.30 p.m. to 1 a.m. is usual. I need seven hours' sleep, and I usually get six.

Does your sleep vary through the year?
No.

Has your sleep pattern changed?
With the baby, it has. I feel like I'm operating on about 85 per cent of my full mental capacity, but I now realise that, post-child, 85 per cent is the new 100 per cent. Fifteen years ago I played Hamlet for 132 performances and got one line wrong. Last summer I played Garry Essendine in Coward's *Present Laughter* for sixty or so performances, and I don't

think I got through a single one of them without a slight hesitation or fluff.

Is the light important?
Very. Much as I like heading out in any weather, it's always nice to greet the dawn and not the darkness.

What do you like least about being awake early?
I can never go back to sleep, so if I've woken before I'd like, the feeling that I'm going to carry this slight fatigue around for the rest of the day is boring. But there aren't any other disadvantages.

What do you like best about being awake early?
I like the space to work, to learn lines. I like the feeling of stealing time. I find my creativity is better and faster. And, being less self-centred, it's the time when most birds are most active: once they've woken up, feeding enough to keep themselves alive for the day is their main objective. So if you want to catch the early birds, you have to be one yourself.

How would you sum up your thoughts on your mornings in 100 words or less?
We aren't born into this world; we emerge out of it, like leaves. When you're a child, you think the world started when you were born. When you have a child, you see that everything up to that point was a part of their creation. The Beatles were right: life goes on within you and without you. The best way I know of tapping into this energy is to get up early.

1 January	10 January	24 January	31 January
Sunrise 8.06 a.m.	*Full moon*	*New moon*	*Sunrise 7.41 a.m.*

JANUARY

January 1

5.15 a.m., Denmark

Another new year on the Danish coast with my Danish wife. Along the bay from her mother. This will be our tenth year wintering here for the holidays. Waking up after Danish New Year's Eve: the sparkling fizz of fireworks, big bangs and booze with friends on the windy beach, watching the moon on unsettled sea. Late to bed. Early up as always. Fire lit, warmth creeping from the stove. I relight the Christmas candles. Wondering what the year will bring.

Later, hoping for hares, I cross the icy decking, crunch the frosted grass to the wood store and stock up on morning logs. The trees sway liquid in the light wind. Sun flickers through the birch and beech like a smuggler's secret code. I spot a miraculous calendula sheltering against the kitchen window, blinking in the low light. I think of these same flowers my brother and I grew together at another garden near another sea. Today we will pack up presents and rye bread. London is calling. Home. But first, when Henri wakes, a walkabout, hopelessly hoping for stirrings of spring.

January 11

5.05 a.m., London

The city blackbird is louder, almost insistent, sensitive to a shift in light it is as yet still hard to see. The sky seemingly dark as ever, though not for as long. Car tops are thick with frost. There is ice on the roof terrace. But the spring equinox is only two months away. The sunrise is earlier and is heading north to its summer home. The birdsong is more urgent. The sirens are too.

January 22

5.25 a.m.

Tulips are picked out in the light of the screen. The sky's almost plain chocolate brown, the moon a fat crescent. There are spots of red on the skyline, the tops of city cranes. A neighbour's crimson-lit window is left over from Christmas. A run of small bright blue lights like a country disco. I wonder who's awake. Just one watercolour window quite far away. I wonder are they sleeping. I wonder who they are. Steam comes off a chimney. A plane passes. The engines' roar starts to whine. I look across to the priory: some priests are awake. Preparing for the old African woman in her bronze-coloured car, always there for early mass. Sometimes her son waits outside. There is a low growl of a night bus as it passes the corner. No one else is moving. I like the unbalanced heat by the window, the streetlight's electric mist.

By 6.30 a.m. there're more cars thrumming, more planes passing. The blackbird's retired. I close the window, it's no longer worth the cold. It's an hour till the bakery opens. I make more tea. A robin picks up the birdsong, others answer. There is dull red on the south-east horizon, the brown is turning blue. The buses now more frequent, more people with places to go, hospital workers to the Royal Free, cleaners up the Hampstead Hill, tired all-nighters trying to stay awake. It is 7 a.m., still no lights, just me and the quiet keyboard. The priory turns its outside lights on. Liam is downstairs, coughing, I make him cold remedy with runny honey, encourage him to sleep.

My morning: Linda Grant

First, could you tell me a little about yourself?
I'm a novelist and before that I was a journalist but I haven't
had an office job since 1988.

What time do you wake up (and why)?
I hardly ever set an alarm, unless it's for an early journey, so
I wake when I wake. In the summer it could be five thirty,
but mostly I seem to wake between six and seven, snapping
out of sleep into full consciousness without grogginess.

Do you have a morning ritual?
I prefer it best if I can wake a minute before six thirty,
because the first thing I do is turn to Radio 3 and I really like
to hear Petroc Trelawny's good morning at the beginning of
the *Breakfast* programme. I stopped listening to Radio 4
several years ago after hearing, day after day from Robert
Peston, that we were facing economic Armageddon and
apocalypse. I decided I would rather face the end in
tranquillity. I subscribe to the iPad edition of *The Times*, so I
look at the news on that and do the easy crossword; if
Petroc is playing something interesting we might have a
Twitter conversation. I have a cup of tea in bed and then
think about getting up.

How does being awake early affect your life?
I can only write in the morning, as close as possible to the dream state, so if I wake late, and particularly if I have something I have to do later, I get very little writing time. Ideally, I like to be at my desk by, say, 7.30 a.m.

What time do you sleep?
Usually I get ready to go to bed at around ten o'clock, but I might listen to a few minutes of the news on *The World Tonight* on Radio 4. I absolutely hate insomnia because it means I wake a bit later, or wake at the same time but less rested.

Does your sleep vary through the year?
Lighter mornings wake me earlier, but if I'm awake before five I try to get back to sleep for another hour.

Has your sleep pattern changed?
Not really, when I was a student I would wake early and go for long walks along the banks of the River Ouse in York by myself.

Is the light important?
Yes, I wake later in winter. I hate that.

What do you like least about being awake early?
Nothing. Nothing at all. I don't even understand the question.

What do you like best about being awake early?
Peace, calm, alertness, silence in the streets.

How would you sum up your thoughts on your mornings in 100 words or less?

Everything is better done in the mornings – work, sex (yes), exercise, answering emails, the shops before they've opened – hence my favourite lines from the popular song, Noël Coward's 'London Pride':

Gay lady, Mayfair in the morning,
Hear your footsteps echo in the empty street.
Early rain and the pavement's glistening.
All Park Lane in a shimmering gown.
Nothing ever could break or harm
The charm of London Town.

FEBRUARY

February 1

5.15 a.m.

Halfway to spring. The blackbird is starting earlier now, in full song in the next few minutes, picking up from the robin. It is noticeably lighter. Easier to sit by an open window, slightly buffeted by a slight breeze and mizzle. It is warmer outside, the forecast is for double figures. The kettle's lit blue as it roars close to boil. It will cut off at ninety degrees. Tea, organic like my veg garden, to be drunk without milk. The birds sing now in stereo. They can sense the change before me.

This time before much of the city, the rest of the house, my family, wake, is when my writing comes more easily. The day shrugs, takes shape. There are flowers on the rosemary, the roof hellebores are in bloom, even the daisies and last year's lobelia. The magnolia buds are furring. Not long now. Still the only light in the streets I can see is from my screen. I want to be sensitive to the change of the day, the month, through the year. Sensitive too to the changes in me.

Even here in the heart of the city, you can feel spring's more urgent pull; the daylight seems more impatient, the soil will be calling soon. It is time to look through seed. Henri is still carrying her injury, so she is sleeping, not practising yoga. At 6 a.m. lights come on in the tower block, early workers wake. The Polish neighbour is stirring. The quiet is being less quietly replaced by movement. People have places to go. The blackbird has moved further away in search of a female. The robin fills its space.

Time soon for the first bath. To start squeezing oranges. Until then, it is just me. Time for a quick read of some news sites, see what has happened since I went to sleep. At 7 a.m. the priory rooms and corridors are lit. The bath is being run downstairs. Time for everyone to wake.

February 4

6 a.m.

Blackbird full-throated, trills over the gardens; planes
cluster over City Airport like bees returning to the hive.
Light clouds scoot past. Canary Wharf looks closer, lit red
and white like a sci-fi city, a kingdom all its own. There is
detritus out the back from a neighbour's party, dead bottles
on the tables, all animation gone. A couple of other early
riser windows blink. The same view at the same time, the
same birdsong. The flashing planes circling, slow, an
occasional descent screams almost politely. There is more
bud and early flower on the window box; this is the one for
cooking: rosemary, thyme, the dormant chive. Crows cry
out their throaty menace. Anemone profiles catch in the
screen light. The sky fractures mackerel blue.

Daybreak looms. There is movement in the church. The
cats are quiet. A crow demands yet more attention. So far
no one is listening, only me. Soon the seagulls will cluster
over the basketball court, a coastal mystery in Kentish
Town. An occasional TV aerial waits for birds, rooftop
relics of an age of two channels. Artisan two-up,
two-downs, transformed by architects and builders,
houses shrugging off their past, adding floors, stretching
out, they grow and flex as their gardens shrink and their
cars get bigger.

There is a yellowing on the horizon, like a fire far away.
The still-dull horizon is lit a little further north. The
chimney pots' profile, fossils from the days of fireplaces,
breakfast tea heated on a range, working men off to work.
The tree silhouettes still wait on leaf. The planes turn up the
volume, less need to be quiet now it is nearly 7 a.m. The
gulls are sounding anxious, maybe lost. The sky shot with
rust and grey, cross-woven like an evening dress. It is almost
morning, sunrise is sooner. The light when it comes creeps
more quickly, almost suddenly it is dull grey like a wintry

seascape, except I can see the brick detail, the white-painted window frames.

February 6

7.20 a.m.

Sky saturated red, sunrise imminent. Sleep fitful. Dreamed about having to dance on stage (I don't dance), with no preparation. Lay awake long before 4 a.m., too early in February, even for me. Finally up just past five, immersed myself in reading. The reds are fading, clouds lit golden like an old picture frame. The trails are straight and criss-crossed so not much wind, chalk lines across the sky, marks on a blackboard from a patient teacher. The tea's cold, oranges are squeezed, Henri bathed, my turn now before the boy. The room has taken a peachy tone.

February 8

4.55 a.m., rested

I like the early-ish nights, not stringing out the time until I am overtired. I limit my social media like I limit the *Today* programme. I try to guard myself against bingeing on everyone else's thoughts, gather mine like mushrooms on a forest floor. Cooler now, a cold snap coming through. I like the bracing chill through the open window. Perhaps the cold connects me to the outside.

The neighbour's cat is calling at the front door. I watch as she crosses the road. Sometimes she waits under cars to check it is safe. By 6.55 a.m. more windows wink, 7 a.m. seems most people's time to get up, wash and dress, breakfast, kids getting ready for school, adults getting ready for work.

February 9
5.25 a.m.

Still. A black cat is silhouetted on a back garden roof, an almost filmic image of night. Suddenly it races. It's seen a blackbird profile. It pulls up short from the tree, turns, back arched, tail fluffed like a cat cartoon. The bird in the top branch continues its song, unimpressed.

February 10
6.10 a.m.

Freezing fog or mist, hard to tell in the dark; cold wet air comes in the open window. The red lights from cranes are invisible now, just a fuzzy couple close to Camden. The blackbird is louder as the mist shuts out the city noise, creates a protective wall, a garden sound studio.

February 13
Sunrise now before 8 a.m.

The sky is almost clear, first time for a week. A few ghost clouds skitting from the east. A pale sun breaks through sometimes. It mirrors the full moon fading from the other window. Four pigeons crowd a TV aerial, as though huddling for warmth, hanging out with mates. Gardens are being cleared, the workmen have finished the neighbour's extension, made rooms for the new baby. Other birds are busying, branches sway. A good day to walk, the first without sleet or rain for a while. It will be eight degrees today. The year zigzags on.

February 16
5.15 a.m.

I walk through the house, sensitive to the shifts in the gloom, almost hearing my way round. A bat man. I feel connected. I light incense. The smoke drifts up, pockets curl and lurk at the bottom of the stairs. Here in the city, it seems there is no such thing as dark. The full moon fading, an ambient, almost invisible glow. It is the same at the Danish summerhouse where streetlights are four kilometres away, the clear sky alive with constellations. It takes adjustment, perhaps trust, before you see depth in the silhouettes. Other senses compensate, eager for the opportunity.

February 19

6.30 a.m.

Slight mist, mostly dark, waiting for the first bus for the first time this year. By the waste bin, a stream of late pee. The air still chill. Only the taxi office alive. A plastic bag hangs lonely from a branch. Blown away. On the bus a couple of clubbers and a couple of workers going home. Another sleeps at the back. A lone building worker with tools dressed for the day. The streets are empty bar an occasional brake light. A worker at the children's A&E looks out of the window. A hospital Edward Hopper. There is a bread delivery at the bakery. A high-visibility man is sweeping the pavement. The last night bus heads towards Golders Green. The only cars are cabs. A woman runs for the Tube, already late at 6.45 a.m. A Christmas tree still lies in the street. Every hundred yards another blackbird. One is singing from a balcony.

At the allotment it's a morning symphony. Robins, tits, blackbirds, the green woodpecker call in 360 degrees. Four ducks fly in formation like on a 1950s sitting-room wall. They turn, change their minds in unison. I pull last year's chard, skeletal, ravaged by pigeons. I sit, look, listen, spot primrose buds in morning dew. The pond is waiting for frogs.

February 21

4.55 a.m.

Woken by the blackbird, impatient now. The equinox four weeks away. Spring forward. British summertime soon. More light, shuddering, new born, slightly unnatural. I will take it, happily. The painted white kitchen floor and table glow like a Turrell installation. Checking a short film on ganzfeld, I stumble on mid-period Dylan. It merges with the birdsong, the window open, the weather mild, spring coiled. I wonder how the broad beans are, the year's first sowing at the weekend, slumbering in still-cold and wet soil, uncurling soon like blind kittens. These (almost) quiet moments are important to me as the day gets slowly dressed. I forage for half memories, feelings, as they ticker-tape through me, watch as they pass like a lazy stream, currents, eddies, maybe fish to be teased out or ignored, my Huckleberry Finn start to the day. Beats being late.

February 25

6.30 a.m., Denmark

Snow. Still winter at the summerhouse. Warm light both sides of the room: an amber glow of sunrise behind me, burbling fire in front. Skies pinking to my left and right, warming the snow. An hour ahead here, daylight already unleashed from dark winter. The dawn race is already won. The stove is roaring, its fire barely contained, flames attacking the glass, fighting to escape. A meditation on movement. The silver birch we planted stand white, almost extensions of the snow. Tracks go through the meadow. I see yesterday's walks to the wood store, the hare's tell-tale footprint. The hedges are all a-twitter; the birds still need help with feeding, sunflower seed and fat balls to be hung in the trees.

By 7.15 a.m. the dawn colours are fading, the blue strengthening, the room warmer. I read by the window.

A different kind of silence invites books. Mostly though the ritual is the same wherever I am: sit, look, listen, the only additional task to feed the fire, check the thermometer, watch its pleasing rise, from ten to twenty degrees before my wife wakes, at home here. We slept a little later last night. Her mother's birthday, with good wine, is why we are visiting.

A new set of trees frame the sunrise; within fifteen minutes the plot is lit yellow, the branches picked out, profiled, the snow reflecting as if from turned-on lights. It's near time for a walkabout though it will have to wait till Henriette wakes. We will marvel at the frosted crystals, try to decipher animal tracks as though we are hunters, talk to the snowdrops, hang out more bird balls.

February 26
4.06 a.m., Danish summerhouse, no stars
Dark of course but not pitch. The east horizon looks alive, like a slight pulse on an injured man. The faintest breath of life. Trees silhouetted, a small grey, a few shades short of the skies to south and west. I stir the ash in the stove, find a few embers, add thin scraps of split log. I blow till it glows. I don't need flame but signs of life: a strand of smoke, a snap and pop of heat to new wood. I close the door and leave it. It will have its own dawn, the red in one corner glows promisingly, same as the grey in the eastern sky. There are no stars. The snow was replaced with rain last night.

I am adept now at making tea in the dark. The metal of the teapot lid a paler shade of grey. The sound of the hot water pouring softens at the top. I stop. I leave it for a few minutes to steep, watch the embers spread in the stove, no flames yet, but the room is a little brighter. The ceiling lamp is picked out like a 1950s flying saucer. There is a streak of something less dark to the south. The fire catches, tears at the wood like a bear with fish. The stove crackles as flames are sucked into the pipe. I top up with heavier logs. My hands smell of smoke as I write, a pleasing thing. The light dies down and the fire takes a second breath, like a hungry man steadying himself; this new log will take time to digest. The room shrinks as the dim light concentrates, sucking the dawn in closer. The more light inside the darker out. Sometimes I light a small candle or two, comfort found in fires and flame.

Today, though, I want to see and feel the shift in an early spring morning. It is March in a couple of days, though spring and summer come later here, a shorter, lighter, brighter season. I take my tea outside and listen to the morning, the constant sea, the trees swaying in an elegant, stately dance. A single hesitant bird call, one note and then it's gone. The rain has brought new wind, new warmth. It's already eight degrees. The pre-dawn perhaps a little brighter, a half shade up on the colour chart.

The logs have aged when I come inside: streaked with grey, their life being sucked into the chimney, their energy leached, collapsing through fatigue. A tree's slow years of growth eaten up inside. The room acknowledges its passing. I pour another tea. There is a poetry here in the near night, a rhythm like a swollen river, eddies of thoughts and feelings, currents caught by the bank. My muse lies here in the morning, smiles. My eyes and ears quicken, my heart and breathing slows. It is peaceful, the almost silence, enveloping like a dressing gown. Cloud has come in, stifled the eastern horizon, an occasional flash, a patch of pale. The teapot handle's lit by the fire, more established now.

The light when it comes is not from the east but all around, dawn like a drawn-back curtain. The birds call in immediate response, different chatter from different trees. The woodpecker lays down a jazz beat on a hollow branch. The birch a streak of chalk on a piece of paper; the oak: charcoal. At 7 a.m. it's grey daylight, cloud cover, drizzled rain. I take a morning walkabout, see new crocus, the runs of snowdrops, daffodils pushing through. The nearby sea sounds windy, birdsong 360 degrees. Time for breakfast soon. The day but not my morning starts when Henri wakes.

February 27
4.15 a.m., London
Pre-dawn. Back at the open window. The blackbird is calling out his territory as I sit in mine. The rain has finally stopped. The city-lit black sky is streaked red. I see my daughter's lights come on in the morning; when she wakes, when she makes breakfast, when her son gets ready for school. I wonder where she's been when she comes in late. At 5.38 a.m. a light comes on in the next street, another in the student tower block. I wonder if they are getting ready to go out or coming in. No lights yet in the church, still waiting on the alarm clock. The streets shine wet and empty. A helicopter roars overhead. Turner clouds streak through, lit from below. A car splashes by. Still the church is dark. The sound of a front door closing.

The neuroscience of sleep and light

In conversation with Professor Russell Foster, director, Sleep and Circadian Neuroscience Institute

What is a chronoytpe?

Your chronotype is determined by your 'natural' sleep pattern (i.e. when you sleep and wake without social, work or other pressure). It was originally used to categorise individuals as 'larks' or 'owls' or neither. Without other obligations, larks will typically sleep from 8 p.m. to 4 a.m., and owls from 4 a.m. to noon. Each account for around 10–15 per cent of the population, with the rest coming in between.

How does sunrise influence chronotype?

Your chronotype is also influenced by the geography of the light–dark cycle where you live. Within the same time zone, there are more larks in the east and more owls in the west. Typically chronotypes are later by the same time as the sun takes to cross from east to west: four minutes for every longitude degree. We think we have overridden the part of our biology to do with seasons, dawn and dusk and the requirement for sleep at a particular time. And of course we haven't.*

How does light affect us?

Before commercialised light and the invasion of the night we were dominated by natural light. The development of mechanical clocks supplanted the natural experience but even twenty years of night-shift work doesn't move the internal clock. It overrides it. The clock is cautious.

What is circadian rhythm?

From the Latin *circa* (about) and *dies* (day). Circadian rhythms help us synchronise to the external world. The suprachiasmatic nucleus (SCN) located deep in the brain enforces a twenty-four-hour rhythm on our biology, anticipating predictable changes in light and temperature as day follows night. These internally generated rhythms permit us to optimise our physiology and behaviour in advance. For instance, before getting up, glucose levels in the blood are going up, blood pressure is rising, levels of alertness are increasing. Later, in anticipation of dusk and sleep, everything is turned around.

* Additional source: *Circadian Rhythms, A Very Short Introduction*, by Russell G. Foster and Leon Kreitzman, Oxford University Press, 2017.

Seven ways to know you're not getting enough sleep

If you are entirely reliant on an alarm clock to wake.

If it takes you a long time to wake up.

If you require caffeine to keep you going through the day.

If you oversleep at weekends.

If you see a big change in your sleep pattern while on holiday.

If you are more likely to remember negative rather than positive elements in your life.

If you don't feel refreshed in the morning.

Seven reasons why we sleep
To package food and store it.
To package toxins and clear them out.
To file information and look at it off-line.
To consolidate memory.
To function well while awake.
To avoid harm.
To conserve energy.

The big question may not be why we sleep, but why we stay awake.

The philosophy of daybreak

In conversation with Professor Barry Smith, director, Institute of
Philosophy, School of Advanced Study, University of London

What does early morning mean?
There is a seventeenth-century Cuyp painting in the
National Gallery of Scotland, *Landscape with a View of the
Valkhof, Nijmegen*, a beautiful Dutch landscape of a tower
in the distance, a river running slowly, figures moving
around in the scene. It is either dusk or dawn. And it is
interesting to look at it and to think, Which is it? To decide
whether it is dusk or dawn. There ought to be about the
same amount of light moments in both cases, yet they are
completely different. The difference is in how you view the
painting and depends on your accompanying internal state,
your physiological reaction.

What is the difference between dawn and dusk?
In one case, the imagined state is of waking, the body is
gearing up to face the day. That response is triggered by the
light source viewed as dawn. You couldn't have that feeling
with the same light quality in the evening. The body is less
rested, less alert.

If it is dawn the figures in the painting are going to work,
alert and alive. There would be a coolness in the air. There
won't be the same light quality in the evening when the
heat of the day is still there, and that might make the light
more diffuse.

We are less intrigued about when we move from day to
night, from light to dark. Sunset is very determinate. Dawn
can never have the same precision. With summer mornings,
there is anticipation of the warmth, of the day. There is the

physiology of coming out of the sleep cycle into the wake cycle. Seeing the light, feeling the body's change in relationship to it, the senses acute and alert. They will be dulled later after a day of being bombarded.

What is the difference between the head and heart?
There is new work by Sarah Garfinkel and Hugo Critchley* on the relationship between the heart and the brain, revealing what the heart knows. Every time the heart beats, it sends a signal to the brain, and those who are able to use this signal will be more attuned to their own emotions and better able to recognise the emotions of others.

Each emotion can have a different cardiac signature. With anticipation the heart rate rises, falls and then levels off, slowing and waiting. Respiratory and heart signals matter. The heart sends a signal to the limbic system before the frontal cortex records them. Some people have a greater ability to tune in to their physical state, are better able to notice subtle changes in their body, feel emotions intensely and recognise them in others. They are more empathetic.

Being more sensitive and alert to the outside world might depend on being more alert and attuned to your internal landscape.

Dawn is just such a time of anticipation, light reaching the retina, triggering the correct circadian rhythms, melatonin levels high. There is an inner and outer resonance, a state of harmony. You can see why many religions would pick that moment of dawn for dedication, the time of re-birth.

Can you cure yourself of lack of sleep?
If you wake early and don't try to fight it; get up at dawn or near it, that is a timeless, rare and special moment. Because there is no one else around, time seems to stop or extend. And it is good for you. You will have one of your better days.

Better than if you try to go back to sleep, and wake up drowsy when the body's chemicals for sleep will flood the system. It is the quiet of it.

Is there a benefit to being awake early?
You have done the dream work: editing, mental filing, sorting while sleeping, so there is a clear channel for new inputs coming in. It is a borrowed secret time. When I get a bit stuck in thought or writing, I will stop, leave it for the next day, then when I wake it is a pleasure, it has been waiting for me, a new beginning for creative thought.

The subtle clues of light, of temperature, of inner bodily state as you rise in the early morning get below the radar. Knowing you are awake when other people are asleep, you almost expand, stretch out in the space. There is a freedom to express the self in a wide, unbounded way.

* Additional source: Sarah Garfinkel, Anil Seth, Adam Barrett, Keisuke Suzuki, Hugo Critchley (2015), 'Knowing Your Own Heart: Distinguishing interoceptive accuracy from interoceptive awareness', *Biological Psychology* 104: 65–74.

Ornithology and the dawn chorus

In conversation with David Lindo, the Urban Birder
(theurbanbirder.com)

When is the best time for the dawn chorus?
For birds, the most vociferous time is spring, from
mid-April until early June, when many are proclaiming
their territories. Especially then, it is the insectivorous birds
that start singing first, including robins and blackbirds. The
seed-eaters come after that. They sing from pre-dawn until
half an hour to an hour after dawn during what they think
is the dead time for insect food. Once the sun rises, they can
get on with parenting and feeding.

Thereafter, it quietens down because they are in full
swing raising their broods. Later in the summer, July and
August, is when most songbirds start to moult. They keep
quieter because they are in poor condition and more
vulnerable to attack. Some are also fattening up so they are
ready to leave.

When's best to see migrating birds?
Migration starts around mid-July. Shore birds are the first to
move. The Arctic summer is quite short. Often the female
leaves the male behind, after having laid her eggs. They are
the first to return. By mid-August, the passerines (perching
birds including songbirds) and other migratory birds are
starting to move. From late August through September the
numbers come through en masse. Numbers swell with the
large number of young. This exodus intermingles with the
arrival of winter visitors.

Around the end of the year, things start picking up for
some species. Robins, for instance, quieten down in later

summer and then start singing again. Their song at this time is often described as more melancholic. This is romanticism, though the song is less vibrant than in spring. The robin is one of the few birds where the female sings as she holds territory. Come November, December, January, they start looking for partners. And start singing more.

For the tawny and other owls it's December to February, maybe March, when they are making a noise because they are in their reproductive scenario. They have their young early. By April they will have reasonably well-grown offspring. This flux goes on the whole time.

What are some of the effects of human intervention?
There is an urbanisation of bird habitat. Streetlights force birds to start singing earlier and louder, competing against the noise of the city. They are not resting. Increasingly, blackbirds sing in the middle of the night in December due to artificial light and the fact that cities are warmer.

Gulls have come into cities. Herring gulls and the lesser black-backed gulls are coastal. The only truly pelagic gull in the UK is the kittiwake, though even that has an urban population in Newcastle upon Tyne. The kittiwake, once they breed in summer, are off into the sea in September until spring: a true seagull.

Gulls started infiltrating western Britain, mainly Gloucester and Bristol, in the 1940s and found the conditions to their liking. Rooftops act as surrogate clifftops. Also, and more importantly, their source of coastal food in terms of fish was diminishing. The populations on the coast are the lowest ever. Herring gulls and lesser black-backed gull are red-listed. Although they may seem common in town – at 4 a.m. you can hear many of them – they are endangered.

Woodpeckers don't sing, their drumming is a replacement. The louder the drumming the more desirable

the males are. In urban areas some males have learned to
drum on metal poles.

Why is dawn important for ornithology?
Mornings, especially in urban areas, are the best time of the
day for enthusiasts. You often get to see birds you'd never
see at another time. Migrant birds are coming in after
making landfall, frantically feeding before they move on or
disappear into the undergrowth. There are very few people
around. It is a special time.

My sleeping habits have evolved over the years. From
mid-March to early July, I wake up by 5 a.m. and then again
from mid-August until mid-November. It is a cyclical thing.

I need to see a horizon. If I am in London I like to be on
my own at dawn with birds at Wormwood Scrubs, four or
five days a week, almost through the year. It is my sacred
time. To see birds fly back to their roost is magical. I feel
cheated if I miss it. It is like Norfolk, the Isles of Scilly, the
Fair Isles, then by 10 a.m. it is a park again. But in the early
morning in the autumn when the mist is low ...

Divine Dawn

In conversation with Canon Christopher Irvine, Canterbury
Cathedral

The monastic link to morning

There was need to have a rhythmic pattern of prayer.
Marking time and marking the year. Their life was geared to
the natural cycle. The timetable was tied to the seasons. Not
just the Christian calendar, but marking day and night.
Christian prayer was influenced by Jewish practice:
working from night through to day, evening prayer to
evening prayer.

The risen son who never sets

With evening prayer came the ritual of the lighting of
lamps. Entering into night with the light of Christ: 'Lighten
our darkness, we beseech thee, O Lord.'

'Early will I seek thee', a line from Psalm 63, greets the
dawn. The appearance of the son who rises and never sets.
This pattern from evening to morning followed what
Christians understood of what God promises: however
dark, however difficult, you enter into the night with
light and in the morning celebrate the victory of Christ
over death.

The beginning and ending

In Ethiopia, an ancient Christian culture, the dawn chorus,
when birds sing in the first light, is seen as a hymn to the
resurrection. The awakening was set out: matins
happened through the night, the service of Psalms and
a reading, units called nocturnes, marking the vigil
towards morning.

Matins was the night office, in the autumn up by perhaps 3.30 a.m. Similar in spirit is the Easter vigil which moves into dawn. Later the pattern of prayer simplified into a beginning and ending: morning prayer and evening prayer, matins and evensong.

Conclusion

The morning in me

This book started as a simple call to wake a little earlier, maybe when the songbirds sing and the sun sits near the horizon. Not every day for everyone. But a small book in praise of dawn and creating a silent place. A call to occasionally free yourself from the demands of work or other obligations. This thing that is the life we lead. A small call to be creative sometime. Time to be yourself.

I have walked and talked with other early risers. Writers and painters and priests. It was not to be a book about packing more work hours into the day, joining the alpha bankers and businessmen at 4 a.m. while the rest of us sleep. It is a piece in praise of choice. Of swimming in the sea at night if you want, standing on a hill at sunrise or quietly reading a book.

I wanted to understand why early morning means so much to me. I spent midsummer in northern Norway and came to know that night isn't the absence of light. There is a morning in midnight sun. You feel it when you walk and watch. It is there when songbirds wake, when wild orchids open, when sea eagles fly. I returned to the far north for the equinox, when days and nights are equal for a moment before the sunrise dies and icy winter wins.

I joined morning prayer as dawn lifted over the Yorkshire hills. I celebrated the new day with Muslim and

Hindu communities. I danced with deities. I sowed seed in the dark, I learned about owls and the dawn chorus. I watched morning bird migration.

I looked at some of the science and philosophy and the spirituality of morning – the three human strands of understanding. I studied a little of circadian rhythms and chronotypes and why I am a 'lark' – one of the 10–15 per cent whose sleep rhythm starts extra early.

I walked with dawn in Denmark, watched swallows dance and saw them disappear. I heard hunters. I climbed sunlit cliffs in East Cork and saw kittiwakes wintering at sea. I sat on an empty beach in Corsica and watched the dawn sea and sky separate.

I spent the night in a James Turrell light installation, observed prayer in a monastery. I came to understand why religions mark this moment. I learned the Christian day starts at night and builds to morning resurrection. I felt the sacred in silence.

Mostly I sat by my window at home at dawn. I looked and listened and learned more of how and who I am. I watched the world wake.

I am not a dawn pied piper urging you to insomnia. I am not calling for you to cut your precious sleep. Perhaps though, sometimes, go to bed a little earlier, get up when the sun does. Give yourself the gift of time. Join the human larks and the blackbirds.

Start with a morning a month, work up to once or twice a week. But try to keep it special if you can.

It has been a year now of waking with the songbirds, of rediscovering home in the dawn. I found freedom in other senses. My eyes and ears have adjusted. I am at home in the dark, maybe more of a fox than a lark.

I have adjusted my sleep, protected myself from ceaseless news and other media. Discovered more about me. Learned to trust. In my instincts, my voice.

I have connected with the natural world outside and inside. I have freed myself from my phone.

I learned to live more in my heart than my head, connected more to feelings than thought. I found peace in quiet.

I am a creature of the dawn, an initiate into nature. I discovered the morning in me.

There is no trick to it, no technique. Except sometimes to go to sleep when you are tired. Try it. Join us. Tomorrow is waiting. Make your morning more magical. If I can do it anyone can.

Twitter and Instagram @allanjenkins21

Early rising: The 20 rules

Try not to turn on bright light. You may not need it. Try to
ween yourself away.

Try to steer clear of email, Twitter or Instagram if you can.
Facebook can wait, so can news. You don't need to
know. Not yet.

Try to listen.

Try to see.

Try to get outside.

Try to be aware of your breathing.

Try to lose track of time.

Try not to do the same stuff you already do during the day.

Try to be creative.

Try to read: perhaps a poem.

Try to write: perhaps a diary.

Try to draw.

Try perhaps to paint.

Try to grow flowers and/or food.

Try to cook.

Try to walk, do a yoga or other exercise.

Try to do the thing you always wanted but 'don't have time
to do'.

Try to protect the opportunity.

Try not to worry at all if it doesn't work out. There is always
(another) time.

Try to remember, there are no rules if no one else is around.

Acknowledgements

First, of course, thanks to Henriette for love, Louise Haines and Sarah Thickett at 4th Estate for encouragement, and to my agent Araminta Whitley as always. Thank you too to Howard Sooley for being a good friend at 4 a.m. and to everyone who answered my early morning questions. Special thanks too to Anne-Marie Hovstadius, the Icehotel, the team at Visit Sweden and to Roddie and Lindis Sloan and the community of Nordskot, Norway, for the loan of their lighthouse. Lastly, my gratitude to David Page, who taught me I might write.

Illustration credits

p. 24–5, p. 38–9, p. 50–1, p. 60–1, p. 72–3, p. 80–1, p. 88–9,
p. 98–9, p. 112–113, p. 124–5, p. 138–9, p. 146–7
Equinoxes, moon phases and sunrise times from London,
March 2019–February 2020

p. 16–17 Sunrise times from London, March 2019–February
2020, drawn by Martin Brown

p. 62–3 The eastern sky in June at 4 a.m. British Summer
Time; approximately 45 minutes before the sun rises, as
seen from Britain © Wil Tirion, Uranography & Graphic
Design

p. 126–7 The eastern sky in December at 7.30 a.m.
± 45 minutes before the sun rises, as seen from Britain
© Wil Tirion, Uranography & Graphic Design